The Best of

Laguna Beach

The best places to dine, drink and play

by Resident Diane Armitage

www.TheBestofLagunaBeach.com • Facebook.com/BestofLagunaBeach

The Best of Laguna Beach

Published by Armitage, Inc.
Laguna Beach, California

Content and majority photography by Diane Armitage with contributing photographers. All photos used with permission.

Book design by Patti Knoles, Virtual Graphic Arts Department
Patti@VirtualGraphicArtsDepartment.com
Glendale, Arizona

Library of Congress Cataloging-in-Publication Data

Armitage, Diane
The Best of Laguna Beach
Unbiased, unpaid recommendations on all the best of Laguna Beach from longtime resident Diane Armitage.

ISBN-01: 978-0-9897929-9-8
Travel
Reference

Printed in the United States of America

www.LagunaBeachBest.com
www.ArmitageInc.com

DEDICATION

For my Laguna BFF, Lisa Childers, who wouldn't let me quit this town.

And, for Ralph and Anita, who wouldn't let me quit this book.

WHAT PEOPLE ARE SAYING ABOUT *THE BEST OF LAGUNA BEACH*

"The Most Comprehensive Guide for Laguna Beach"

"This is the only book you'll every need to navigate around Laguna Beach. I read it cover to cover and think it's the most comprehensive guide that has ever existed in this town. Well done!" – T Burns

"My Go-To Book"

"This is my go-to book when deciding which of the many Laguna Beach restaurants and events to visit or recommend to visitors and guests. I've lived in laguna Beach for 15 years and still haven't been to all these great places! Well-written and fun to read!" – Erika Lemmon

"Invaluable to Tourists and Longtime Residents Alike"

"As a 30-year resident of Laguna Beach, I find this book to be a great find. Well laid out, beautiful photos and down-to-earth, honest comments about place to eat and things to do. This book is invaluable not only to tourists visiting our wonderful little town, but to longtime residents as well." – R. Jameson

"This Book Helped Me Plan My Entire Wedding Weekend in Laguna"

"After visiting Laguna Beach once years ago, I always wanted to get married there. Eventually, I set the date but then had no idea what to do or where to turn for guidance on restaurants, retailers and events that might be occurring while my family and guests were here. This book came to my rescue in a big way, AND I got online with the author, Diane, and she helped me even further. Needless to say, everyone is still talking about the most amazing time they had here in Laguna Beach. You really made it special, Diane." – K. Merritt

"This Book is an Absolute Gem."

"Locals and well as visitors will not only benefit but enjoy this absolute gem. If you really want to know what to do in this fabulous town of ours, this is the most practical (and humorously well written) guide you'll need. Find out the top restaurants, best dishes and then what to do in Laguna after your fabulous meal!" – L. Childers

"I Keep Buying This Book for My Clients – and They LOVE It"

"Every time I have a client come to meet with me here in Laguna Beach, I purchase Diane's book for them and send it in advance of our meeting. They LOVE it. As soon as they arrive, they're ready with suggestions for me as we spend time in Laguna, and we're always over-the-top pleased with Diane's suggestions. There's just no book that even comes close to sharing Laguna Beach as we really live." – M. Stanton

"One Great Review and Tip After Another"

"Diane ... what a great job you've done in giving the visitor and local the spin on what's good and where, exactly, it is. Your book is one great review and tip after another on what's going on in this small town of Laguna Beach. Fantastic resource!" – R. Flores

TABLE OF CONTENTS

photo credit: Mike Altishin

FOREWORD

In 1995, I was engaged to a guy who wasn't very nice. I believe that every person comes into your life for a reason, though, and his reason had to do with introducing me to Laguna Beach. He brought me to the Surf & Sand Resort on New Year's Eve 1995, and on New Year's Day, I wrote a "resolution" that I would eventually move to Laguna Beach. Even in that short, overnight visit, I knew I'd come home.

I moved here in September 2000, and have been avidly exploring this town ever since. In 2008, I decided to start writing a blog about what to do and where to go in Laguna Beach. At that time, someone asked me what in the world I would write about. Wouldn't I just run out of material? I chuckled then and I still chuckle now – Laguna Beach is the most creatively active, magical town I've known. Every day in Laguna Beach is a new story and a new discovery. We locals love to talk about what is and what is to be and, apparently, at ***LagunaBeachBest.com*** now, many thousands of other people are interested in the same!

This book is a culmination of all my hundreds of blog entries.

I don't call myself a "food writer"– I'm just a regular person looking to enjoy a great experience. I think I've been lucky enough to get to know a lot about the greatness of this town that most visitors (and even some locals) don't get a chance to experience, and I want you to love this town as I do.

I've never asked the restaurants or events to comp or give me "freebies." In fact, I've made a point of remaining as anonymous as possible because it's important that I experience exactly what you would experience. Further, over these initial blogging years, I haven't asked for ad dollars from any of the entities I've written about because I don't want you – my reader – to feel that I might have been swayed in some way.

Lastly, I don't review franchises or large chains. Although I have nothing against these entities, I think the local restaurateurs and merchants here put all their talent, money and sweat equity on the line to take care of you, and they deserve to have larger audiences because of that commitment.

OK, so all that being said ... **What if your own entity – or the entity you love and adore – isn't in this book?** Because this is based on my ongoing blog, you are reading a portion of an ever-evolving "Laguna Beach's Best." If a favorable review isn't here now, there's a chance it will be in the next year's revised edition.

But, clearly, in the end, this IS "the Best of Laguna Beach." If food is inconsistent, it doesn't get in the book. If the experience is a flat line, and my local friends feel the same, it doesn't get in the book. If the service is rude, arrogant or lacking, it doesn't get in the book. Fellow tourists might have given it 4 stars at Yelp ... but if the Laguna Beach locals don't go there, I'm going to steer you to places and events we love, instead.

The way I see it, we all work hard for our money, and we all want to have a great experience, especially in a new town we've chosen to visit or reside. We deserve to be treated like gold, period. (Not entitled. Just well treated.) Happily, most of Laguna Beach knows how to do just that with a style and grace I've rarely experienced elsewhere.

Now it's your turn.
Welcome to my beautiful town.

RESOURCES FOR YOUR VISIT

Who knew that my idea to just get out of my house and start exploring this beautiful Laguna Beach town would lead to this? Thanks to the 20,000+ subscribers now at www.LagunaBeachBest.com, and thanks to the thousands of readers who have purchased this book and joined us at Facebook.com/BestofLagunaBeach, I can assure you … I receive hundreds of questions and "what's the best for ... (fill in the blank) queries each and every month.

I love that you're out there. For starters, it assures me that you've all come to recognize that what I'm recommending is not paid advertising in any way, shape or form. When I think it's the best, I write about it, period.

Secondly, it assures me that Laguna Beach is a sought-after vacation destination for people all over the world, and this makes me very happy. And, third, your questions have helped me innovate, create and seek out solutions for you so that your time here in Laguna Beach is the most awesome time you've yet experienced.

So, consider this section a "resource" section for your greater involvement in Laguna Beach –

- Trip planning
- Fantastic Culinary Adventures for groups
- The most talented photographer to have at your side
- Free shuttles to get you through town
- And, yes, the most requested of all requests – DOG love.

HOTEL ACCOMMODATIONS

North Laguna Beach
North Laguna entrance to Broadway (Main Beach)

Arabella Laguna • 506 N. Coast Highway • (949) 376-5744
Art Hotel • 1404 N. Coast Highway • (949) 494-6464
Crescent Bay Inn • 1435 N. Coast Highway • (949) 494-2508
Inn at Laguna Beach • 211 N. Coast Highway • (949) 497-9722
Laguna Cliffs Inn • 475 N. Coast Highway • (949) 497-6645
The Tides • 460 N. Coast Highway • (949) 494-2494

Downtown
Broadway to Cleo St.

14 West Boutique Hotel • 690 S. Coast Highway • (949) 715-4840
Hotel Laguna • 425 S. Coast Highway • (949) 494-1151
Hotel Seven4One • 741 S. Coast Highway • (949) 494-6200
Pacific Edge • 647 S. Coast Highway • (949) 494-8566
Sunset Cove Villas • 683 Sleepy Hollow Lane • (949) 376-5396

The Village
Cleo St. to Cress St.

Holiday Inn Laguna Beach • 696 S. Coast Highway • (949) 494-1001
Laguna Riviera • 825 S. Coast Highway • (949) 494-1196
The Retreat in Laguna • 729 Gaviota Drive • (949) 376-7170

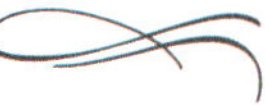

South Central
Cress St to Montage Resort Drive

Best Western Plus Laguna Brisas Spa Hotel • 1600 S. Coast Highway • (949) 497-7272

Capri Laguna • 1441 S. Coast Highway • (949) 494-6533

Casa Laguna Inn & Spa • 2510 S. Coast Highway • (949) 494-2996

La Casa del Camino • 1289 S. Coast Highway • (949) 497-2446

Laguna Beach Inn • 2020 S. Coast Highway • (949) 494-5450

Montage Laguna Beach • 30801 S. Coast Highway • (949) 715-6000

Seaside Laguna Inn & Suites • 1661 S. Coast Highway • (949) 494-9717

Surf & Sand Resort • 1555 S. Coast Highway • (949) 497-4477

Travelodge Laguna Beach • 30806 S. Coast Highway • (949) 499-2227

South Laguna
Wesley Drive to South Laguna Beach entrance

The Ranch at Laguna Beach • 31106 S. Coast Highway • (949) 499-2271

CONCIERGE HELP: PLAN YOUR LAGUNA BEACH VACATION

Read More: www.LagunaBeachBest.com
Contact: Diane Armitage, Diane@LagunaBeachBest.com

Beautiful Laguna Beach, photo credit: Mary Hurlbut, MaryHurlbutPhoto.com

Diane Armitage and her team are Laguna Beach's "go to resource" for singles, families, couples and groups. Our personalized services are suited to each distinguished client's unique interests.

With Laguna Beach's Best V.I.P. Concierge Services, you have the opportunity to be pampered "V.I.P. style" with a personalized plan that features the very "best" of Laguna Beach.

Perhaps you're bringing valuable clients to Laguna Beach. You might be planning a pre-wedding weekend for your bridal party. Maybe you're bringing your family to town and want to add in more than just hanging at the beach. You might be wining and dining your potential spouse ... or your company's potential board president. (If you're bringing a group to Laguna Beach, see our Custom Culinary Adventures, too!)

Whatever the case, and whatever the story, we not only bring your wants to fruition, but provide only the "best" recommendations, reservations and tickets for your Laguna Beach vacation. Whether you want help planning your entire itinerary or just need help with a few specifics, we charge very reasonable rates to get you dialed in to the very best of Laguna Beach.

Among the many services we provide:

Accommodations

- Luxury Home Rentals
- High-End Vacation Rentals
- Bed and Breakfast Recommendations
- Laguna Beach Hotel Accommodations

Dining

- Dining Reservations & Chef's Table Reservations
- Private Chefs
- Nutrition Coaches

Activities & Events

- Custom Walking Tours
- Event Ticket Procurement
- Family Entertainment
- Golf Tee Times
- Health & Fitness Options
- Live Music & Clubs
- Personal Trainers
- Spa Services & Reservations
- Surf, Skimboard and Stand Up Paddle Lessons
- Surrounding Area Event Tickets & Theme Park Tickets
- Tennis Coaching & Reservations
- Tidepool Tours

THE BEST OF LAGUNA BEACH CULINARY ADVENTURES

Read More & Complete a Culinary Request:
www.LagunaBeachBest.com/Group-Dining-in-Laguna-Beach

Treat your group to a customized culinary adventure! Laguna Beach Best plans creative culinary events for your most memorable, innovative group dining experiences in Laguna Beach.

We know every culinary entity in Laguna Beach, and excel at working with these culinary artists to create custom, fun events. Why bother with hundreds of ads or random Yelp reviews when we can easily direct you to the best experiences for you and your group?

We help groups averaging between 6 and 16 people enjoy ...

- Catered events with live entertainment
- VIP wine dinners
- Dining "tours"
- Parties featuring wine, cognacs and rum tastings

Go to our website at www.LagunaBeachBest.com/Group-Dining-in-Laguna-Beach to complete our no-obligation request form. Just give us your details and we'll start the magic!

photo credit: Mike Altishin

PHOTO STEWARD: DOCUMENT YOUR TRAVEL

Request the Photo Steward: www.LagunaBeachBest.com/Contact-Us

You might snap a hundred photos on your trip to Laguna Beach, but how many of those photos can be enlarged beautifully and framed over your fireplace or on your kids' walls?

Mike Altishin, the "Photo Steward of Laguna Beach" handles that for you. A native of Southern California and a resident of Laguna Beach, Mike is a third generation photographer, having been inspired by the life documentation his grandfather did (the "first photo steward").

Mike's passion and desire to photograph and document travel and adventure was cultivated at an early age, and he maintains that easy-going enthusiasm as he captures friends, couples and families in "natural poses" while they take in the life of Laguna Beach.

FREE SHUTTLES

Laguna Beach can be an absolute cluster of traffic, pedestrian crossings and endless circling for parking spaces.

Heaven forbid we chase you away from the glorious town of Laguna Beach, so our little city came up with a great Free Trolley Service a few years ago.

Now, nearly all year long, we have a huge number of trolleys trundling along the separate routes – North, South Aliso Creek, South Laguna and the Canyon for the major festival centers.

We have you covered from every boundary of the town, and you can easily transfer between the routes. Tourists and locals alike regularly pack on to these cable car look-alikes and, while the ride may not always be a fast breeze through town, at least you're not driving (and stuck dead cold) in the snarl of it all.

Trolley stops reside at practically every block and are scheduled about every 20 minutes (high traffic times might see a bit of delay, but these drivers really have it going on). The trolleys run from 9:30 a.m. to 11:30 p.m., so no worries about cutting your dinners short or running from the Pageant before its evening curtain call.

Drive to a lot, take the shuttle from there.
Try to take advantage of the city's primary parking lots and you can shuttle from there without worrying about your meter expiring (our meter maids and men take their jobs VERY seriously, trust me).

Central downtown lots –
The Lumberyard lot (adjacent to City Hall on Forest), and the Mermaid Street Garage are available during weekends and evenings. One of the more popular lots for you early birds is at Glenneyre between Laguna

Avenue and Legion Street. Parking at smaller, private lots is also available in the downtown area.

South Laguna lot –

There's a small parking lot at 3rd and PCH on the ocean side. The Mission Hospital has also expanded parking options in its covered parking structure at 8th and PCH.

The Canyon –

The city also offers an expansive "Act V" parking lot in the Canyon at 1900 Laguna Canyon Road (also known as Highway 133). From Main Beach, it's 1.3 miles up the canyon, past the primary festival grounds.

DOG FRIENDLY RESTAURANTS

Laguna Beach is extremely dog friendly. The beaches allow dogs on leashes, even during certain summer hours, and just about every retailer in town is welcoming to dogs. If every restaurant could have a patio, they would likely all be obliging to dogs as well.

The list that follows covers all of the restaurants we've managed to yet find that allow dogs on their patios.

For the finer dining establishments, please call ahead to ensure that there will be room for your dog on busier nights.

Adolfo's Mexican Food
998 S. Coast Highway, Laguna Beach, CA 92651 • (949) 497-2023

Anastasia Cafe
460 Ocean Ave, Laguna Beach, CA 92651 • (949) 497-8903

Andree's Patisserie
1456 S. Coast Highway, Laguna Beach, CA 92651 • (949) 494-1577

Avila's El Ranchito
1305 S. Coast Highway, Laguna Beach, CA 92651 • (949) 376-7040

Brussels Bistro
222 Forest Avenue, Laguna Beach, CA 92651 • (949) 376-7955

The Cliff Restaurant
577 S. Coast Highway, Laguna Beach, CA 92651 • (949) 494-1956

Dizz's As Is
2794 S. Coast Highway, Laguna Beach, CA 92651 • (949) 494-5250

Eva's Caribbean Kitchen
31732 S. Coast Highway, Laguna Beach, CA 92651 • (949) 499-6311

GG's Bistro
540 S. Coast Highway, Laguna Beach, CA 92651 • (949) 494-9306

Gina's Pizza and Pastaria, North Laguna
610 N. Coast Highway, Laguna Beach, CA 92651 • (949) 497-4421

Gina's Pizza and Pastaria, Main Laguna
1100 S. Coast Highway, Laguna Beach, CA 926511 • (949) 494-4342

Heidelberg Pastry & Bistro Shop
1100 S. Coast Highway, Laguna Beach, CA 92651 • (949) 497-4594

Hennessey's Tavern
213 Ocean Ave, Laguna Beach, CA 92652 • (949) 494-2743

Husky Boy Burgers
802 N. Coast Highway, Laguna Beach, CA 92651 • (949) 497-9605

Koffee Klatch
1440 S. Coast Highway, Laguna Beach, CA 92651 • (949) 376-6867

Laguna Coffee Co.
1050 S. Coast Highway, Laguna Beach, CA 92651 • (949) 494-6901

La Sirena Grill, downtown
347 Mermaid Street, Laguna Beach, CA 92651 • (949) 497-8226

La Sirena Grill, South Laguna
30862 S. Coast Highway, Laguna Beach, CA 92651 • (949) 499-2301

Laguna Feast
801 Glenneyre Street, Laguna Beach, CA 92651 • (949) 494-0642

Lumberyard
384 Forest Ave., Laguna Beach, CA 92651 • (949) 715-3900

Madison Square Garden & Café
320 N. Coast Highway, Laguna Beach, CA 92651 • (949) 494-0137

Maro Wood Grill
1915 S. Coast Highway, Laguna Beach, CA 92651 • (949) 793-4044

Nea Politan Pizzeria
31542 S. Coast Hwy, Laguna Beach, CA 92652 • (949) 499-4531

Nirvana Grille
303 Broadway St., Laguna Beach, CA 92651 • (949) 497-0027

Ocean Ave Brewery
237 Ocean Avenue, Laguna Beach, CA 92651 • (949) 497-3381

Orange Inn
703 S. Coast Highway, Laguna Beach, CA 92651 • (949) 494-6085

Papa's Tacos
31622 Coast Highway, Laguna Beach, CA 92651 • (949) 499-9822

Ristorante Rumari
1826 S. Coast Highway, Laguna Beach, CA 92651 • (949) 494-0400

Romeo Cucina
249 Broadway St., Laguna Beach, CA 92651 • (949) 497-6627

(The) Rooftop (Casa del Camino Hotel)
1289 S. Coast Highway, Laguna Beach, CA 92651 • (949) 497-2446

Sapphire Laguna
1200 S. Coast Highway, Laguna Beach, CA 92652 • (949) 715-9888

The Stand
238 Thalia Street, Laguna Beach, CA 92651 • (949) 494-8101

Sushi Laguna
231 Ocean Ave, Laguna Beach, CA 92651 • (949) 376-8786

Taco Loco
640 S. Coast Highway, Laguna Beach, CA 92651 • (949) 497-1635

Zeytoon
412 N. Coast Highway, Laguna Beach, CA 92651 • (949) 715-9230

Zinc Café & Market
350 Ocean Avenue, Laguna Beach, CA 92651 • (949) 494-2791

Life in Laguna Beach

My God-Dog, Bindi

Dining at its Best!

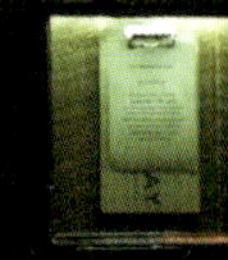

Broadway by Amar Santana

328 Glenneyre St. • Laguna Beach

Broadway by Amar Santana
328 Glenneyre St. • Laguna Beach

BROADWAY BY AMAR SANTANA

328 Glenneyre St., Laguna Beach, CA 92651
Reservations recommended: (949) 715-8234

Dinner average $16 – $36
Hours: Sun – Wed 5:00 p.m. – 9:00 p.m.; Thurs 5:00 p.m. – 10:00 p.m.
Fri/Sat 5:00 p.m. – 11:00 p.m.
Corkage fee: $25
Noise level at busiest: 6 out of 10
Good for kids? No
Dogs? No

Menu: www.LagunaBeachBest.com/Menus/Broadway-Restaurant

In downtown Laguna Beach, the restaurant, *Broadway by Amar Santana*, is manned by an extraordinary chef.

To the uninitiated, the restaurant might sound oh-so-haute, but Chef Amar is the farthest thing from "haute" imaginable. He sits across the table from me, hunkered on his elbows, grinning like a 10-year-old boy.

With his story, who wouldn't grin? Raised as a poor kid in the Dominican Republic, he moved to New York with his family and, shortly thereafter, remembers watching a biopic of famed Chef Charlie Palmer. "He was driving down the Las Vegas Strip in a convertible, smoking a cigar," says Amar. And I thought ... man, I want to be THAT guy!"

Fast forward 10 years through a high school cooking program he initially dropped out of ("Who wants to COOK for a living?") to a full-ride scholarship to CIA in New York, and Amar tells the serendipitous tale of being hired for his internship ... by Charlie Palmer, himself. Amar became a master chef for Charlie Palmer and opened restaurants in the man's behalf for the next six years. He only left Palmer to open his own restaurant in 2012 here in Laguna Beach.

"I don't have a convertible, but, yes, I have driven down the Las Vegas Strip smoking a cigar in my BMW," Amar says, with a wide grin.

We're not sure if the 31-year-old Amar ever stops grinning. And we're not quite sure when or if the guy ever sleeps. Amar doesn't do things that other chefs do. Take, for instance, his new Charcuterie Board on the Broadway's newly updated menu. Charcuterie boards are popular items these days. Most chefs order up a few sausages, add a couple fine cheeses, and call it a day.

Chef Amar, on the other hand, lays down an 8-piece board of sausages, pâtés, and truffle-y mousse, each of which he's crafted, smoked and cured meticulously by hand ... on a whim. He just "kind of came up with each one." Here's Duck Salami, Hungarian Smoked Sausage, Pork Rillette, traditional Kielbasa, Pork Liver Paté, Smoked Truffle Chicken Liver Mousse and, finally, his new take on Porchetta di Questa.

And Chef Amar is just getting started.

Broadway's Ever-Changing menus

Amar says he looks forward to debuting his new menus so much that he can't limit himself to just one new update per season. Expect almost monthly changes.

Of course, they can never remove the Brussels Sprouts from the menu. Amar does a quick calculation and figures the Broadway sells approximately 1,100 orders of Brussels Sprouts each month. As if by osmosis, a waiter appears with the magical bowl, a sublime meld of crisp, roasted Brussels with Chinese sausage slivers and sweet chili sauce "with about 20 added herbs and spices," admits Chef Amar.

"Only two people have the recipe for the Brussels Sprouts," Amar says with his usual happy smile. "...The dishwasher and me."

The best-selling Mediterranean Branzino is staying, too, and the Grilled Prime Skirt Steak will remain as well. As we discuss Ahmed's pension for the Branzino (flown in fresh from Greece or Spain), Chef Amar appears with his Stuffed Braised Artichoke. He sits next to me to pour the sauce, tableside. He is grinning all the while.

I expected an ... artichoke. You know, the big bulb with all the leaves you peel and scrape with your teeth. Chef Amar is appalled. "Why would I make you do all that work?"

General Managing Partner Ahmed Labatte pairs the artichoke with a beautiful glass of Esporao, White Reserva from Alentejo, Portugal, and we talk wine. When the Broadway first opened, it boasted 130 wines. Now, the restaurant

offers 400 selections of wines, the broadest list in Laguna Beach next to the Montage. Oddly, Laguna locals happen to like tawny ports and dessert wines, so the restaurant has expanded that index handily. Ahmed's careful selections have earned Wine Spectator's prestigious "Award of Excellence."

For other entrées, Chef Amar adds a Tomahawk Pork Chop with dried apricots and cipollini. The Free Range Chicken is spruced with asparagus and lemon risotto. For the vegetarian-minded, he is reintroducing his meatless Wild Mushroom Bolagnaise, created with smoked tofu, fava beans and dried and fresh mushrooms. Diners nearby tell me it's "unworldly."

For me, all thoughts of Bolagnaise trip from my head as the Skirt Steak is presented. It is grilled to perfection, bedded in a caramelized onion jus whose consistency is just slightly thicker and shinier, almost a glacé. A swirl of Chimichurri sauce (an Argentinian creation of puréed parsley, oregano, chilies and olive oil) proves a perfect dipping partner to the meat. It is, frankly, one of the best steak dishes I've ever eaten.

The ambience here at the Broadway is spectacular. Great music is playing, new cocktails are pouring, the captains and expediters are fluidly moving, and Chef Amar moves from table to table, chatting and grinning. I smile as I watch him circle his room and think, "What a happy relief he decided to cook for a living."

At Press Time: Chef Amar Santana Expands To Second Restaurant
695 Town Center, South Coast Plaza in Costa Mesa

In summer 2015, expect the opening of Chef Amar's second restaurant themed as inspired traditional Spanish cuisine at South Coast Plaza in Costa Mesa. Watch LagunaBeachBest.com and search 'Vaca' for updates.

CAFÉ ZOOLU

860 Glenneyre St., Laguna Beach, CA 92651
Reservations HIGHLY recommended and well in advance:
(949) 494-6825

Dinner, average $15 - $32
Hours: Tue – Sun 5:00 – 10:00 p.m.
Corkage fee: $15
Noise level at busiest: 7 out of 10
Good for kids? Yes but keep in mind – this is a very small place. Rambunctious kids could be ejected by nearby diners.
Dogs: No

Menu: www.LagunaBeachBest.com/Menus/Café-Zoolu

Definitely in my Top Four Restaurants of Laguna Beach, Café Zoolu is a wonder all its own. For starters, the place is dinky. Owners Toni (hostess and main waitress) and Michael (head chef) Leech have managed 18 years in this tiny cottage with an offering of, maybe, 8 seats at the bar where Chef Michael cooks, and an allowance for about 25 diners at the tables.

Chef Michael has been at this 40 years, both in Hawaii and here on the mainland. This must be a case of "practice making perfect" because I'll tell you here and now, this guy does not miss a beat on anything he produces.

Michael and Toni met while he was the Executive Chef at Five Crowns in Corona del Mar, and that, too, was a long, long time ago. She's the edgy, funny, no-nonsense front man (Toni once made Barbra Streisand stand outside on the sidewalk in the rain because her handlers hadn't made a reservation for Zoolu's busy Valentine's night). Michael, meanwhile, is the guy with his head down, turning out phenomenal dinners all the night long with his famous mesquite broiler relentlessly firing.

Michael calls his food "Cali-Polynesian" which, when pressed, he claims is a mix of Hawaiian, Asian, Mexican and Cajun influence. Let me say again very clearly: It doesn't matter which national heritage you choose to make your plate at Zoolu's … whatever you choose will have you waving its country's national flag by evening's end.

"Best in the World"

Anyone and everyone will tell you that Michael's Baseball Swordfish (actually more the size of a softball) is the best in the world.

If swordfish isn't your game, there are plenty of other seafood and fish dishes on the menu, including other best-sellers Soft Shell Blue Crab, Alaskan Salmon and Laguna's own Spiney Lobster in season (Oct – March). For me, I've never had Cioppino on Bouillabaisse like Café Zoolu's anywhere in the world. This fresh seafood stew is packed, with swordfish, ahi, mussels, clams, scallops and shrimp AND sits on a bed of pasta. It's drama, man. And don't even think of passing up the Calamari Asian Style for your appetizer.

If at least nine different kinds of nightly fish just aren't your game, have no fear. With the Zoolu Meatloaf actually able to rock your socks off, you know you can't go wrong with Michael's superb Filet Mignon (I'd vote this best in Laguna Beach), his Grilled Pork Chops, Osso Buco, or Penne Rigata. And that's just for starters. The Café Zoolu menu is bigger than the restaurant itself.

Top it all off with Michael's "Expresso Crème Brulée, his sublime Jasmine Rice Pudding, or his fresh-baked Warm Brownie topped with mint chocolate chip ice cream, hot fudge, whipped cream and mint liqueur.

I guess part of the charm of Café Zoolu is that it's so far removed from being a well-run franchise of a place. This is a real-life husband-and-wife team who make it happen six nights a week. They put roots down in Laguna Beach decades ago and they're here to stay. In fact, before the Montage Resort broke ground in 2001, we locals remember that extensive stretch being Treasure Island, home to 268 trailers. Toni and Michael owned one such trailer and, after the Montage was built, they figured out that a couple bar stools at the far west end of the Montage Lobby Bar were in direct position over what used to be their living room. So, on just about every Monday evening, the couple sits in their "living room" to enjoy a couple drinks.

That, my friend, is what I love about Laguna Beach. Enjoy the spirit of Café Zoolu.

The Driftwood Kitchen
& Stateroom Bar

photo credit: Driftwood Kitchen

DRIFTWOOD KITCHEN & STATEROOM BAR

619 Sleepy Hollow Lane, Laguna Beach, CA 92651
Reservations Recommended: (949) 715-7700

Dinner, average $16 – $38
Hours: Dinner 5:00 – 10:00 p.m., Stateroom bar, 5:00 p.m. – midnight (daily breakfast and weekend brunch also served)
Corkage fee: $25, 2 bottles
Noise level at busiest: 5 out of 10
Good for kids: OK, but they're apt to get fidgety
Dogs: No

Menu: LagunaBeachBest.com/Menus-Driftwood-Kitchen

At one point in our Laguna Beach history, the Beach House was our grand dame restaurant, serving thousands of meals in an old world setting. Even though the girl grew tired in her last years, there was a great gnashing of teeth from the valiantly loyal when she closed her doors.

The day Chef Rainer Schwarz and partners John Nye and Colby Durnin stepped in to create their new idea here – Driftwood Kitchen – they knew they had very big shoes to fill. Happily, when you step into the new Driftwood, you suspect they've already met their goal.

In Through the Out Door

The Driftwood experience begins with actually stepping through the front doors of the restaurant rather than the backside of what the Beach House customarily used. Now, when greeted at the top of The Deck stairs (their other restaurant, see page 134), you're led through the revamped "living room" to the actual restaurant side of Driftwood. The mere shift in entry is, frankly, breathtaking.

photo credit: Driftwood Kitchen

"I wanted THIS to be your first impression," says Nye with a sweeping gesture that takes in white walls and beams and towering windows framing ocean and sky.

If anyone remembers the old Beach House with its dark restaurant interior, it seems the Driftwood Kitchen's wall space has shrunk, while its windows have dramatically increased in stature. Not so. The walls and the windows are exactly the same dimensions as they were before. This is an historical property – the new management wasn't even allowed to replace the glass panes of the existing windows. Somehow, though, it is an amazingly different vibe.

Now, let's get back to the bar, renamed "The Stateroom." While the partners first thought they'd shift the bar to a lighter concept, in the end they embraced the beautiful dark wood of the original edifice. The team also added a glorious copper bar, a substantial line of high-end whiskeys and scotches, and updated the back patio with couches, Adirondack chairs and a fire pit.

Created for the "Locals' Palates"

While The Driftwood Kitchen is an elevated experience, both literally above The Deck and figuratively with a more expansive and exotic menu, Chef Rainer prefers to call The Driftwood an "elevated casual" restaurant. "Laguna residents don't need pretentiousness or stiffness," says Chef. "But they *do* possess sophisticated palates. Food is a big thing in this town."

If anyone knows how to innovate a "creative" menu, it's a Chef who's been doing this for more than 30 years. Chef Rainer was initially an apprentice at the age of 15 in an Austrian castle that had been converted to a fine dining restaurant. He has since devoted his life to steering a multitude of global restaurants to greatness. And, once involved in the Driftwood renovation, Chef says his new menu evolved in similar manner.

photo credit: Driftwood Kitchen

Take, for example, one of his favorites – Chef's Texas Redfish. "Most times when restaurants serve whole fish, they do grouper or catfish and it's always tasted flat to me," says Chef. "So, I choose Redfish or Branzino, which are both super moist fish, and then we add all sorts of flavored oils and herbs before flash-frying the entire fish."

New Takes on Fresh Tastes

On my visit, we tried a sampler of the Lobster Bisque (light and flavorful) and a gorgeous Caprese Salad, comprised of a towering stack of thick Heirloom tomato slices sandwiching creamy Buffalo mozzarella and basil leaves with a grilled plum at the crown.

photo credit: Driftwood Kitchen

Then, it was on to the Hawaiian Ahi, flash fried, dredged in Ponzu sauce and served with pickled vegetables. The Atlantic Halibut filet showed up next with fingerling potatoes, corn fricassee and English pea sauce. Delectable, not a flaw in any of the servings.

"The goal here was to give this beautiful restaurant back to the locals in all its glory," says Nye. "And, with what Chef Rainer is doing with the food, we think our regulars will be as proud of the effort as we are."

K'YA BISTRO

1287 S. Coast Highway, Laguna Beach, CA 92651
(in La Casa del Camino hotel)
Reservations recommended: (949) 376-9718

Dinner, average $4 – $10
Hours: 4:30 – close
Corkage fee: $15
Noise level at busiest: 7 out of 10
Good for kids? Uhmmm ... this is a friendly place, and I've seen plenty of kids here, but they can get fidgety
Dogs? No

Menu: www.LagunaBeachBest.com/Menus/Kya-Restaurant

When people ask me about my very most favorite restaurants in Laguna Beach, I mention four. This one – K'ya Bistro on the lobby level of the Casa del Camino hotel – is one of them. In fact, I'd even go so far as to say it's in my Top Two.

Mention K'ya Restaurant to locals and "foreigners" and the response is the same: "What's it called?" It's K'ya. Pronounced: "Hi ya!" About 8 years ago, Chef Craig Connole (who is probably the most relaxed, non-chef-acting chef I've yet met) took over Savoury's. He quickly introduced an entirely new menu that he describes as "Pacific Asian with some Nebraska thrown in." And, after the economy took its first hit in about 2009, Craig shifted the ENTIRE menu to small plates.

About 70 small plates to be exact.

That's right. I said 70 small plates, all priced between $4 and $10. And for the record, food arrives on a small plate, yes. The servings, however,

are far from small. Most can be easily shared.

Now, some people look at this enormous menu and feel immediately overwhelmed. Take heart. Just look and point – it's all quite fantastic. Somehow, the gifted Connole has managed to create a truly memorable eating experience in everything he puts on this menu, from "Snacks" (Chicken Empanadas, Smoked Salmon Potato Cakes and delectable Sweet Potato Fries) to flatbreads, at least 10 inventive salads, and the largest line up of soups you'll find anywhere in Laguna Beach.

And Chef Craig's just getting started.

Craig's fish and seafood dishes include the must-have Hawaiian Ahi Poke and Flash Fried Calamari in Thai Glaze (this isn't like any Calamari you've ever experienced in your whole, entire life).

This portion of the menu also features hearty cuts of Hibachi Salmon, Cajun Shrimp, Grilled Portabello & Lobster, and more!

If fish isn't your style, just mosey on over to six or seven pastas (Lobster & Truffle Risotto, oh my). Or, take a gander at the rambling meat and poultry aisle of K'ya's small plate menu decadence, including Grilled Lamb Chops, Chicken Marsala, Short Ribs and hefty gourmet burgers. We ask how he does it. Nobody can answer. We ask how his kitchen is able to come up with all these dishes in their tiny little apartment-sized kitchen. Nobody can answer that either.

The restaurant itself is a bustling, somewhat crowded place. Don't expect to show up on a busy night with hopes of having a quiet, romantic dinner. There are a lot of happy, chatting people here. Your first visit to K'ya will have you pretty darned happy, too.

LUMBERYARD

384 Forest Ave., Laguna Beach, CA 92651
949-715-3900

Dinner average $12 – $33 (Lumberyard also serves Sunday brunch)
Hours: Mon – Friday, 11:30 a.m. – midnight, Sat & Sun, 11:00 a.m. – midnight
Noise level at busiest: 5 out of 10 in restaurant (without live music), 2 out of 10 on patio
Good for kids? Yes
Dogs? Allowed outside of patio

Menu: www.LagunaBeachBest.com/Menus/Lumberyard-Restaurant

In early 2008, many Laguna Beach long-timers felt some trepidation when their beloved Cedar Creek Restaurant closed shop at this prime location at 384 Forest Avenue. We tiptoed close and craned to look

through the shrouded windows to see what all the hammering and racket was about, and wondered aloud what local architect Gregg Abel was up to in there.

When the Lumberyard threw its doors open in October 2008, we were all in for a surprise - it wasn't even close to the same place. Of course, now that we know Cary Redfearn, the proprietor, we understand why. Cary has devoted his entire life to the restaurant world in about every position possible. After opening many, many restaurants for various corporations, he began owning his own restaurants, the most recent before the Lumberyard being the venerable Oysters in neighboring Corona Del Mar.

Changing up a restaurant in a 1916 historical building had its challenges for Redfearn and team, but the result was a beautiful nod to this building's first use as the city's lumberyard. The historical place offers plenty of table seating, but the Lumberyard's got to have one of the biggest saloon bars in town, surpassing The Marine Room and Laguna Beach Saloon.

Enough on the character and atmosphere. Let's get to the food.
First, let's remember that Executive Chef Armando Ortega has been creating high-level foodie delicacies since the early Oysters days more than 17 year ago. Together, Redfearn and Ortega opened the Lumberyard with a sizable menu that reflects what discerning diners came to expect at Oysters.

For starters, Ortega's Cedar Planked King Salmon is unstoppable, and he also offers Parmesan-Crusted Sole, Roasted Halibut with an asparagus shrimp risotto, and a seared Sea Bass over truffled potatoes (deadly). Of course, the freshest raw oysters are also perfectly prepared when the season allows.

The Lumberyard offers more steak options than most Laguna Beach restaurants. Or, try the Boneless Short Ribs or Babyback Ribs. And

innovative pasta dishes are only usurped by the Crowned Champion of Comfort Food ... the Lumberyard Chicken Pot Pie.

For "lighter" fare, the Lumberyard has invented a number of signature dishes, including its Lumberyard Planks (flash-fried zucchini planks with lemon aioli dipping sauce), a memorable Ahi Tartare stack, Dungeness Crabcake salad (easily my favorite salad in all of Laguna Beach), and its famed signature burger.

Let's not forget the famous Hog Heaven Pie. (I don't know if they made up that "famous" part but I've tasted this deadly chocolate ganache/ peanut butter mousse creation and, yes, it deserves to be famous.) *See Snacks and Desserts for a photo.*

The service is friendly. Not an ounce of snobbery here. The pours of wine are a full one-third glass (250 ml!), which we think is darn right nice of them, and the draft beer options are extensive.

MARO WOOD GRILL

1915 S. Coast Highway, Laguna Beach, CA 92651
(949) 793-4044

Dinner average $16 – $32
Hours: noon – 9:00 p.m. Tuesday, Wednesday, Thursday and Sunday, and noon – 10:00 p.m. Friday and Saturday. Closed on Monday.
Noise level at busiest: 5 out of 10 in restaurant, 2 out of 10 on patio
Good for kids? Yes
Dogs? Yes

Menu: www.LagunaBeachBest.com/Menus/Maro-Wood-Grill

If any of you are familiar with the term "Mercury in retrograde," you'll understand why the espresso machine broke down at Maro Wood Grill on Tuesday.

When I arrived on Tuesday to chat with Mariano "Maro" Molteni and his Chef, Debra Sims, Maro was up to his elbows in coffee grounds as he tinkered with the dratted machine.

When I showed up to take photos the following day, a smelly asphalt truck at a nearby business was pluming its asphalt smoke directly into Maro's patio. I found the entire restaurant crew huddled inside with every door and window closed, and Chef Debra talking sternly to whipped cream that was melting too quickly for our photos in the closed quarters.

Whatever the planetary skew or whipped cream mishap, though, Maro and Debra are endlessly cheery and vibrant. She's trying new menu recipes. He's planning a lamb grilling event on Saturday. As well-suited business partners, they love running one of the most successful restaurant "secrets" in town. And, with all the Maro Wood Grill menu items organic and sustainable, the delicious fare is only more appreciated by the restaurant's throngs of fans.

Argentina Comes to Coast Highway

Maro Wood Grill opened in September 2011 after several months of retrofit construction of the former A La Carte catering business. Based on Maro's Argentinian roots, the Grill opened up a whole new world of organic, wood-grilled delight to Laguna's foodie palate.

"The problem with Argentinian, wood-grilled food is that there are just so many options," says Chef. "The food is so clean and so good, you just can't stop at a single menu."

So, she doesn't. Every single week, Chef Debra creates at least three or four new menus, and posts them on the *MaroWoodGrill.com* website almost every morning.

Initially, Chef Debra started with prix fixe menus on certain days of the week, and you will still find that theme in her "Supper Specials" on Friday and Saturday nights. (This week, the Supper Special is Grass-fed Baseball Steak with Roasted Potatoes, Mesquite Blue Lake Beans and Coconut Pecan Ice Cream Sandwiches.)

"The other nights of the week, I just change it up, based on new ideas and the fresh produce and protein we have coming in that day," she continues. "We want this to be the freshest food experience, and that really requires daily attention to our menu offerings."

And then, of course, the 29th of every month is reserved for Gnocchi Night. "It's a real crowd pleaser," she says with a grin. "The flavor changes every month, depending on the seasonal vegetable I have available."

Given the restaurant's cozy square footage (9 people inside, 30 outside), it's no surprise that this restaurant fills regularly with reservations, especially on the weekends.

Happy, Grass-Fed Beef

Despite Chef Debra's penchant for change, there are tried-and-true favorites that will never be removed. Were she to remove the Maro Wood Grill Burger from the menu, for instance, crowd riots could ensue. The burger is the restaurant's best seller at lunch and dinner.

Another crowd favorite is the Grass-Fed Skirt Steak, a resident on the Maro Wood Grill menu since the restaurant's first day of business. Now, normally when it comes to skirt steak, cooks and chefs know it has a tendency to be a bit chewy or tough, but Chef Debra's is a melt-in-your-mouth experience. "It's a happy cow," says Chef Debra with a shrug. "Grass-fed beef is the healthiest, smartest choice in beef because it's how they're naturally raised."

The skirt steak arrives with a cheeky portion of chimichurri, which I'm initially reluctant to try because the steak is so darned good on its own. The chimichurri, though, adds a perfect accompaniment, as it's made of parsley, garlic, red onions, rice vinegar, red wine vinegar, canola oil, crushed red pepper and salmuera (a salt and water combination).

So New, It Doesn't Have a Name

This week, Debra is working on a new beet salad dish. It doesn't have a name yet, but it's already won a place on the menu, this I can assure you. Grilled and shredded red and gold beets join shredded carrots

and radish. She's added her house-cured artichoke hearts, but thinks something is still amiss, so her house-cured asparagus spears are the next addition. She tastes it and nods approval. "They have just the right amount of cumin to bring up the flavors of the entire dish," she says.

Atop the pile of salad, she adds two organic (Laguna Beach grown) 4-minute eggs, then drizzles her Lemon Thyme Vinaigrette as the crowning touch.

"It's earthy and crispy and sweet with a little bit of tang," says Chef. "And the eggs add this great richness to the dish."

Yep. This no-name beet salad is a definite keeper ... as is Maro Wood Grill in the Laguna Beach landscape.

NIRVANA GRILLE

303 Broadway Street, Laguna Beach, CA 92651
949-497-0027

Dinner average $22 – $36
Hours: 5:00 p.m. – 9:00 p.m. Tues – Sunday. Closed on Monday.
Noise level at busiest: 4 out of 10
Good for kids? Yes
Dogs: Yes

Menu: www.LagunaBeachBest.com/Menus/Nirvana-Grille

Lindsay Smith-Rosales might very well be the only chef in Laguna Beach who actually was born and raised in our fine town. For this very fact we should all be extremely grateful, as Lindsay is serving up one of the finest menus at our own Laguna beach-based Nirvana Grille.

"My Mom was a vegetarian caterer so we grew up cooking everything from scratch and using sustainable foods long before the word

photo credit: Nirvana Grille

"sustainable" was even a word anyone knew," says Lindsay. While Nirvana Grill boasts all sorts of meats, poultry and fish, even Chef Lindsay's richest sauces and preparations are normally gluten free, and refined sugars are kept to the barest minimum across the board. Nirvana is also one of the few restaurants in town that produces an entire gluten free menu (see their website), and Chef readily accommodates vegetarians, pescetarians, dairy-free folks and vegans.

Nirvana To Be Back in Hometown Laguna

After graduating from culinary school, Lindsay quickly routed her way to the Ritz Carlton in Laguna Niguel, where she not only improved her chef skills but also met her soon-to-be husband, Luis.

The couple opened their first successful Nirvana Grille in Mission Viejo in 2006 and, after ongoing discussion about returning to her Laguna roots, Lindsay and Luis signed papers for their new location in early 2008.

Truly Innovative Appetizers & Salads

Chef Lindsay has worked from Day One on creating a warm, approachable environment that mirrors the same in its menu offerings. "We want people to feel like they're dining in a good friend's home ... a good friend who cooks really well," Chef says with a laugh.

Nirvana's best sellers include the Roasted Poblano Chile in the appetizer section. Never one to pass on spice, I had to try this unique (and rather monstrous) chile.

"My chefs suggested I add a spinach artichoke dip to the menu, and I wasn't very excited about that," says Chef. "So, I came up with this idea of making something that was less ground up and with less cream involved and then stuffing the chile with the concoction.

The "concoction" is downright yummy. An entire chile is served open face, stuffed with fresh spinach, artichoke hearts, shallots, a bit of cream and Parmesan cheese. It's served with homemade cheesy bread, a take on neighbor Cindy Gray's great cheese bread from Lindsay's childhood.

Of her many creative salads, I choose Chef's Burrata and Organic Heirloom Tomato Salad, which also shows up at the table constructed completely differently than any other similarly named salads I've tried. I'm treated to a beautifully arranged rabble of Kalamata olives, small puffs of gorgeous burrata cheese and cherry-sized heirloom tomatoes tossed in a basil pesto and balsamic reduction.

Entrees Break the Usual Mold

While nearby regulars assure me that I've missed out by not trying the Sea Bass or, at the least, the Surf and Turf specialty, I'm more than blissful with my lamb dish. It is perfectly done and all around heavenly.

Sadly, there are few chefs who treat Rack of Lamb with the respect and love it deserves. Chef Lindsay, though, is all about big love on this dish. Chef coats the lamb with a mix of finely chopped pistachio nuts, white wine, Dijon mustard and a small bit of panko. She finishes the rack in a rosemary demi glace.

After all the many restaurants I've enjoyed in this town of ours, it's one of the few that provides a high level culinary experience with so much inviting warmth and friendliness. Then again, what else would you expect from a Laguna Beach native?

RISTORANTE RUMARI

1826 S. Coast Highway, Laguna Beach, CA 92651
Reservations recommended: (949) 494-0400

Dinner, average $14 – $44
Hours: 5:30 – 10:30 p.m. daily, closed Mondays
Noise level at busiest: 5 out of 10
Good for kids: Not really
Dogs? No

Menu: www.LagunaBeachBest.com/Menus/Rumari-Restaurant

My good buddy from Denver, Don, is back in Laguna Beach for his weekly stay-of-the-month at his condo. This means I get to go to Rumari's Italian Restaurant again. Until Don started hanging more regularly with the Laguna Beach wanderer here, Rumari's was the ONLY restaurant he would visit on every trip out.

Initially, I wasn't terribly excited about Rumari's. I'd eaten there a few times in my early years in Laguna (like 2000), and felt it was a bit inconsistent. He was appalled at my commentary and insisted I give it another try. So, now that I've been to Rumari's at least 10 times, I really do owe this fine establishment a retraction. This is a great Italian restaurant.

Just like the other stellar Italian restaurant in Laguna, Romeo Cucina (see next page), Rumari's is owned by Italians, RUN by Italians and SERVICED by Italians. These people aren't messing around.

(On that note, it seems that even if you can trace your family lineage to seven-generation Sicilian, you probably won't get to sit at the bar. For the last year, each time Don and I have ventured into the establishment, our favorite option of sitting and eating at the bar is usurped with several "reserved" signs at just about all of the seats. Apparently, these lucky few "reservees" are part of an unwritten code that we haven't yet cracked.)

Even Rumari's setting is old school, sophisticated Italian

Rumari's dining room offers over-stuffed bench seats and chairs, white linens, and chandeliers dripping in yards of glass baubles.

This is fine Southern Italy and Northern Tuscany dining. Some of my local friends protest at the entrée prices but, seriously, Rumari's menu pricing is equaled by the likes of 230 Forest, Watermarc, Tabu Grill and more. Were it simply serving up spaghetti and meatballs, that would be one thing, but Rumari's serves up items such as Nero Linguine Seafood (a deadly combination of black linguine pasta in foil with clams, tiger shrimp, tomato sauce and brandy), Grilled Veal Chops (either served with shrimp in a white wine porcini mushroom sauce or with garlic and rosemary in a chianti demi glace), or three options of Laguna Beach's most succulent Filet Mignon dishes.

If you manage your way through the overwhelming wine list by the bottle … and if you manage through the over-sized main entrees … you've GOT to get the ice cream dessert, Semi Freddo. Rumari's version of a hot fudge sundae, this vast improvement on the subject proffers vanilla bean and white chocolate chip ice cream with a shot of hot fudge, a shot of espresso and a crumbled amaretto cookie to top the torture. You just can't tackle this dessert without grinning like a school kid.

ROMEO CUCINA

249 Broadway St., Laguna Beach, CA 92651
Reservations recommended: (949) 497-6627

Dinner, average $12 – $28
Hours: Mon-Fri, 5:00 p.m. – 10:00 p.m.; Saturday & Sunday, 11:30 a.m. – 2:30 p.m. and 5:00 p.m. – 10:00 p.m.
Noise level at busiest: 4 out of 10
Good for kids: yes
Dogs? On patio

Menu: www.LagunaBeachBest.com/Menus/Rumari-Restaurant

Vincenzo ("Enzo") Romeo is the kind of guy you like instantly. Walk into his restaurant, Romeo Cucina on Broadway, and you might as well have walked into the kitchen of his own home.

Having been born above his father's restaurant, Enzo doesn't see that your restaurant experience should really be any different than actually eating in his home. Raised with six brothers and sisters in Vibo Valentia in southern Italy, the siblings were working in the restaurant and learning their first recipes from Mom and Dad before they had graduated grade school.

Fast forward a few decades and a hop across the Big Pond, and Enzo and brother, Antonio, are still dishing out Mom's recipes, Dad's baking secrets and their own concoctions in this Romeo Cucina ("the kitchen") location for 23 years. (Twenty-three years!) This is just one of two Romeo Cucinas (the other is in Laguna Niguel) after a long line of successful Italian restaurants in L.A., Palm Springs and Corona del Mar.

"We make everything here in our kitchen two to three times a week," says Enzo. "All the tortellini, pastas, raviolis, breads, and the majority of our desserts ... and we still make Mom's meat sauce and tomato sauce the way she's always made it."

While Mom Romeo, now 84, still insists on cooking Sunday's entire family meal for a brood of 15-20 people, Enzo and Antonio insist on being in the kitchen every day of the week to ensure they're providing "family meal" love to a bevy of longtime regulars and new visitors.

Romeo Cucina's Food — Like the Home You Wish You'd Grown Up In

Recent changes and additions to the Romeo menu only make your decision more difficult. The brothers have added new appetizers to an already-substantial list, a hearty new salad to join five others, and at least 12 new dishes in the extensive offering of pastas, "secondi" entrées and wood-fired pizzas. Additionally, Romeo Cucina offers gluten free pasta and pizza crusts as options.

In some cases, the new dishes are a fresh take on an old classic. Take, for instance, Romeo's popular Bruschetta Piatta, now served as flat focaccia bread baked in their wood oven and topped with just-picked tomatoes, garlic, basil and ricotta salata.

For the first time in forever, I'm not wrangling with a big chunk of bread and can actually taste the super-fresh toppings. It's absolutely lovely.

Nearly a Century of Family Cooking at Italian Village Pricing

As it's impossible to "taste test" an assortment of hearty pasta dishes, Enzo decides to cook up four mini versions of new dishes and old favorites for me. Given that I'm a sucker for Italian food, but a self-professed foodie fanatic, too, I feel that I've died and gone to heaven when the plate arrives.

The Gnocchetti alla Grappa lightly coats homemade potato pillows in grappa sauce with chopped bits of zucchini, sun dried tomatoes and mushrooms. (You might know me as a self-professed foodie fanatic, but I'm also a closet gnocchi maker – I haven't easily found gnocchi that's light and fluffy, so I've always resorted to making it myself. Happily, I think I can now retire the rather tedious task and call in the order to Romeo Cucina.)

Turn the plate counterclockwise, and it's two more "taste testers," Panzarotti D'Aragosta nestled next to a separate serving of Artichoke Ravioli. In contrast to the Gnocchi's mildness, the Ravioli dish is a rollicky burst of garlicky artichoke, capers and lemon ladled over raviolis stuffed with sublime mascarpone and ricotta cheeses. As I'm the kind who will eat capers from a jar, I adore the contrast of tang and salt with the creamy cheeses. It's a riot of flavor and fun.

Moving right along, it's on to the Panzarotti, a freshly made stuffed pasta that resembles a miniaturized half-moon ravioli. In this case, the pasta is stuffed with fresh, local lobster ("Aragosta"), and crab meat, and then tossed in a tomato sauce of fresh shrimp and scallops. With its super rich meld of flavors, it's small wonder this is one of the restaurant's perennial best sellers.

Finally, I eye the last dish for tonight's taste test, Tortelloni de Carne.

It's so gorgeous, I had saved it for last, but now wonder how I'll even manage two bites.

The homemade tortelloni is plump and perfect and filled to the brim with tender rib eye. Tossed in today's fresh pesto sauce and garnished with arugula and shaved Grana Padano, it's a bases-loaded homerun hit outta the park. (I manage four bites and beg for a to go bag.)

Romeo Family Enjoys Extended Family

As the Romeo family specifically chose Laguna Beach in 1988, they think of the Laguna locals as none other than their extended family. "My brother was the first to arrive from Italy, and he was in L.A., and I didn't really like L.A.," says Enzo. "So, one day he called me and said, 'I found the town for us,' and I flew out, came to Laguna Beach with him, and decided that week to move my family from Italy."

Though he started cooking in Beverly Hills, it didn't take long for Enzo to gather the family wagons and venture to their agreed preference in South Orange County. Enzo says they feel an affinity for Laguna as it has that "Euro feeling," he says.

"Laguna Beach is a lot like Portofino – it's like living every day on vacation by the ocean," says Enzo. "And all the art and the people who live here ... it's our kind of village."

SELANNE STEAK TAVERN

1464 S. Coast Highway Laguna Beach, CA 92651
Reservations recommended: (949) 715-9881

Dinner, average starters $12 – 18, entrees $34 – 46
Hours: Closed Monday; Tues – Thurs, 5:00 p.m. – 11 p.m.;
Friday & Saturday, 5 p.m. to midnight; Sunday, 5:00 p.m. – 11:00 p.m.
Corkage Fee: $15
Noise level at busiest: 5 out of 10
Good for kids? No
Dogs: No

Menu: www.LagunaBeachBest.com/Menus/Selanne-Steak-Tavern

It was a blessed relief to every local in town when Selanne Steak Tavern finally opened in the old French 75 space.

The renowned French 75 was a beloved spot for decades, and Selanne had its share of trials moving its innovative menu and concept into that historic landmark building. But, just as its namesake has soldiered on to become one of modern hockey's greats, the restaurant vanquished every obstacle to finally open in November 2013.

Any time a new restaurant opens in Laguna Beach, it tends to be placed under a hot, stern spotlight. Even with the beloved Anaheim Ducks

Teemu Selanne at the helm, the Tavern has endured its share of scrutiny.

Having dined at Selanne Steak Tavern three times now, I'd say the greatest advantage the restaurant team enjoys is its chefs' attention to superb foodie detail. Before the restaurant opened, I met with Executive Chef Josh Severson, Sous Chef Randall Hane, and Pastry Chef Heather Fisher. In a world of many older, more well-known chefs, I have even greater respect for these three as they started in this industry as young, wet-behind-the-ears wanna-bes and remained absolutely committed to creating at the highest levels of foodie heaven.

The Foodie Food at Selanne's

Severson and Hane are *quite* the innovators with favorites I've tried such as Severson's "Signature" Pacific Diver Scallops, the Scarlet Beet Ravioli stuffed with a decadent blend of goat cheese and hazelnuts, the Beef Short Rib that simply melts in your mouth, and the all-vegetarian Forest Mushroom Risotto.

photo credit: Selanne Steak Tavern

Don't even get me started on Heather's pastry skills. For starters, she's so danged cute you just want to hug her for no explainable reason. If I could have a daughter (beyond my beloved almost daughter, Lacey), I'd vote for Heather in a minute. But, as adorable as she is, she's one serious pastry chef, the talents of which we don't see often in this town of ours.

photo credit: Selanne Steak Tavern

Heather is at fault for my happy increase in overall body fat with her Apple Pie in a Jar, Sticky Toffee Pudding and, most recently, her fresh-baked Monkey Bread, a deadly combo of sticky buns, warm caramel pecan drizzle and maple ice cream. I hate her and I love her. Ha.

Selanne Pulls Off Hat Trick

Every new restaurant has its occasional bumpy takeoff points but, for the most part, Selanne Steak Tavern has done a fine job in hiring the right personnel to take on the scrutiny and pressure.

Selanne Steak Tavern has filled very big shoes and expectations, and they stand to have a long and happy relationship with Laguna Beach for years to come.

STARFISH ASIAN CUISINE

30832 S. Coast Highway, Laguna Beach, CA 92651
Reservations recommended: (949) 715-9200 or online

Lunch & Dinner, average $8 – $22
Take Out Hotline: (949) 715-8205 (large party takeouts also available)
Delivery also available, Three Arch Bay to Emerald Bay
Hours: *Lunch*, M-F 11 – 4 p.m.; *Dinner*, nightly from 5 p.m.
Noise level at busiest: 4 out of 10
Good for kids? Patio is more amenable. The interior restaurant is a bit more formal, although I have seen plenty of kids.
Dogs: No

Menu: www.LagunaBeachBest.com/Menus/Starfish-Restaurant

The first time you visit Starfish Asian Cuisine in the Haggen's parking lot across from the Montage, you're in for a shock. On the outside,

you figure, "It's a shopping strip kind of restaurant." As soon as you walk inside, though, the gorgeous, decadent décor is only outdone by the phenomenal food and service.

In a recent Laguna Beach Restaurant Week write-up, I noted that Starfish was in my Top 5 restaurant recommendations against the other great Laguna Beach restaurants participating. I'd safely say, though, that Starfish is definitely ranked in my Top 5 Restaurants in ALL of Laguna Beach. These people just don't miss a single beat.

Managed and owned in a 4-way partnership between Gretchen Andrews (formerly GM at Tabu Grill), Archie McConnell and Marco Romero (both longtime PF Chang's General Manager and Executive Chef, respectively), and a small cadre of silent partners, Starfish is what I call "the little South Laguna restaurant that could."

It started with the South Laguna residents loving the place, and this is the most important hurdle to conquer. As one such South Laguna peep, I can attest that we love our quieter lifestyle down here (a whopping 3 miles from Laguna's Main Beach center), but we haven't had any real place to hang out (sophisticated bar-wise) or dine in foodie fashion (except Eva's Caribbean). We locals needed a neighborhood eatery and friendly bar that eased somewhere between sit-down dining and loud bar scene.

Why Starfish is in my Top 4 in Laguna Beach

Starfish was a winner from Day One, and it only got better when Gretchen brought in Archie and Marco to solidify and enhance an already-great menu. You might venture to say that Starfish has a "PF Chang's" kind of menu but – for the record – I would never choose to eat at PF Chang's at least once a week, and I have to physically STOP myself from eating at Starfish every night of the week. It seems that the change for McConnell and Chef Romero was a spectacularly freeing one as Starfish produces stellar, consistent food.

For me, I always eat at the bar, and recommend that others do the

same (if you don't have kids along, of course). The restaurant seating is divine, and the newly created patio is its own oasis, for sure, but the bartenders at Starfish are such a cut above the rest in friendliness and professional efficiency that I rely on their nightly recommendations of drink AND food as much as I would a sommelier's pick on Pinot Noir.

When I'm with friends, we order up larger servings such as their Pan Seared Pork Dumplings, the endless offers of fantastic fish dishes (Mahi Mahi "Hot Fish"seems to be the presiding favorite), or the towering Jenga-like stack of the meatiest, tastiest 5-Spice Baby Back Ribs you've ever experienced. (See my Starfish "Opium Hour" Happy Hour, too, page 181)

It's interesting how a restaurant takes on a life of its own. Much like its namesake, Starfish is a charming and comfortable place for tourists and locals alike, and South Laguna finally has a local watering hole to call its own.

Tabu Grill
2892 S. Coast Highway • Laguna Beach

TABU GRILL

2892 S. Coast Highway, Laguna Beach, CA 92651
Reservations recommended: (949) 494-7743

Dinner, average starters $12 – 18, entrees $34 – 46
Hours: Every night, 5:30 p.m. – 9:30 p.m.
Corkage Fee: $15
Noise level at busiest: 7 out of 10
Good for kids? No
Dogs: No

Menu: www.LagunaBeachBest.com/Menus/Tabu-Grill

There's a new chef in town and he's already shifting it up at our cozy foodie restaurant, Tabu Grill.

Long known for her rich and innovative menu of Polynesian and Asian influences, Tabu Grill has had the reputation as a "special event" restaurant with long waits to even be allowed in its doors.

Chef Kenny Raponi is changing all that. "We're not dropping our food quality whatsoever," says Chef. "But, we're changing things up to create more menu and happy hour items, and we're introducing amenable menu specials that bring people in on a regular, weekly basis.

"The key is to continue providing the rare thing we're known for – that sweet and savory combination we pour into all our dishes – but with a wider range of portion and pricing options so that Tabu becomes more of a regular stop for our community residents and commuters heading home every night."

Take, for example, the Sea Bass Chef Kenny serves me on my afternoon visit. The broth spooned into the dish's base is a slow-cooked mix of miso, truffles and soy. He adds a lightly sautéed mix of asparagus, purple cauliflower and salsify in soy yuzu. Atop that he layers the sea bass. And atop the bass, he adds candied kumquats, orange segments and Upland cress.

Breaking into Chef Kenny's gorgeous plating of any dish is the hardest step to take. Fortunately, I was able to break on through for a thoroughly enjoyable meal of Sea Bass. The meld of flavors he achieves in this single dish is pretty darn close to spectacular.

New Chef is the Old Chef

Bringing Chef Kenny in – who actually worked at Tabu Grill three years ago for a little over a year – was a lucky break coupled with sheer effort to get him behind the Tabu line again.

"Kenny knows our Tabu style and he created a lot of what's still in the list of favorites on Tabu's menu," says Tabu Partner Chuck Bixler.

"He's got a rare talent for food and a great business head – he knows how to run a kitchen. When the opportunity came up for a new chef, we started hunting Kenny down. It took us a while, but it was certainly worth the effort."

Menu Change-Ups at Tabu

Chef Kenny talked his favorite Sous Chef, Scott Jansen, into relocating from Northern California, and in just a few short weeks the two have tackled the Tabu menu.

Many menu items, like crowd favorites Ahi Poke or Beet Salad, are enjoying minor changes (i.e., the salad's accompanying goat cheese baklava will likely shift to blue cheese). More creative plating with zigs and zags and arcs of new, fresh sauces and salsas will also be in play (i.e., the Poke has a great Sriracha and sesame arc of triumph on the plate).

Other changes afoot:

- Duck is moving into place instead of chicken.
- Daily house-made pot stickers are likely to be replacing the gnocchi. The once-popular Flat Iron Steak with decadent macaroni and cheese is being returned to the menu.
- A 12-ounce Pork Chop is joining the menu, its "savory" combined with the "sweet" of Chef Kenny's honey grits.
- Meanwhile the Pork Belly dish shifts slightly to an "Asian braise" with garlic, ginger, lemongrass and other unpublished ingredients.
- And, the Mahi Mahi will sit atop its own earthy vegetables with an Asian brown butter gastrique that incorporates garlic, ginger, green onions and more. And the soups and sorbets. Well. For the record, the soups and sorbets at this place just keep getting more amazing.

When I visited this week, Chef Kenny ladled out an Asparagus Vichyssoise and topped it with a delicate sauté spoon and drizzle made of corn, shallots, garlic, lemon juice and jalapeno. He topped it with the tiniest sprig of scallion (who has the patience for this placement?) and then expected me to destroy it with my spoon.

Eventually, no matter how beautiful the dish, you simply have to give in. The food is just too good here.

Finally, my last word of advice – with soups and sorbets changing every few days, you simply must order both every time you visit. About a week ago, I dropped in for a Tabu Trio Sorbet and was treated to three hearty scoops – Sweet Corn, Thyme Basil and Cucumber Mint. Seriously? Each one was off the charts.

Valet Parking, No Reservations

While Chef Kenny adds new life to the kitchen, management is working to create a more amenable, easy front, too, by introducing complimentary valet parking. Tables are normally available any night of the week, even on a walk-in basis. Tabu has a no-reservations policy at the bar during happy hour as well as a no-reservations policy on the outdoor patio all night long.

"People have this concept that it's impossible to get into Tabu Grill," says Managing Partner Tom Burns. "Yes, we have busy nights and we might do occasional buyouts for holiday parties or wedding receptions, but those nights are rare. We want people to say, 'Hey, why don't we head down to Tabu Grill?' and know there's a place for them here."

Reminder: Tabu Grill DOES have a happy hour, Sunday through Thursday, 5:30 – 6:30 p.m., with a complete menu of food and wine options that doesn't scrimp.

Further, the weekly changing Chef's Tasting Menu – also Sunday through Thursday and priced at just $29 for a 4-course prix fixe menu – should prove to be even more interesting now that Kenny and Scott are at the helm.

"It's a great way to introduce our guests to items they might not have tried or new menu items that give them a hint of what's coming around the bend," says Chef. "And it keeps us fresh, too."

Frankly, I'm not sure how that would happen, that whole 'we could lose our freshness' thing. It's a fun kitchen and a new energy at Tabu Grill. I don't see the "fresh" wearing off any time soon.

242 CAFÉ FUSION SUSHI

242 N. Coast Highway, Laguna Beach, CA 92651
Reservations highly recommended: (949) 494-2444

Dinner average $11 – $20
Hours: Sun – Thurs, 4:30 p.m. – 10:00 p.m.; Fri/Sat 11:30 a.m. – 10:30 p.m.
Noise level at busiest: 7 out of 10
Good for kids? Yes
Dogs: No

Menu: www.LagunaBeachBest.com/Menus/242-Café-Fusion

When I think of 242 Café Fusion Sushi, I think of Harry Potter's train station platform at 9 and ¾. If you blink, you'll miss it completely. But oh, if you discover it and clamber inside, you're in for a whole new world of foodie discovery.

This is by far the best sushi I've ever eaten anywhere. 242 Café Fusion Sushi is a teeny tiny restaurant run by one of the only female sushi chefs around (and she's teeny tiny, too). But the sushi here is huge … huge in serving, huge in texture, huge in flavor. We're talking haystacks of sushi here, folks, not prim little pieces atop a chunk of white rice.

Above all else,

Chef Miki Izumisawa believes in balance. She wants you to experience sushi with all five senses (sight, touch, taste, sound and smell). As you gather in a place that accommodates nine chairs at the bar and six small tables, you feel as if you've been invited to a dinner party in someone's home. "Golden daily specials" are printed and passed from table to table on a gold-lacquered plate – pay attention, as these are the beginning of the memorable "haystacks."

Miki is happy to serve up single pieces of sushi and she has a decent list of "General Rolls" whose names you will see offered in other sushi places. But, Miki prefers to create "haystack" combinations or hefty hand rolls that arrive at your table in a bountiful, carefully arranged piece of heaven. Take, for example, one of her bestsellers, the Sexy Hand roll ... it's fresh spicy ahi tuna, shrimp and scallops melded with mint, avocado, crunchy potato crisps and cilantro.

My favorites:

- The Moon & Sun Fusion Sashimi ... a combo of seared tuna, salmon, yellow tail, white fish, shrimp and smelt eggs with a spicy olive oil/soy/vinegar sauce to accompany.
- The Father in the Sky – salmon, spicy tuna, crab, smelt eggs, pickled radish, scallions, sesame seed and Romaine lettuce
- The Lava Flow – spicy tuna, salmon smelt egg, crab, avocado, red chard and macadamia nuts with a soy onion garlic sauce
- Sunshine Snow – yellow tail, white fish, albacore, tuna, salmon, scallion, sesame seeds, Serrano chilis and lemon served up with ICE CREAM!

You won't be served soy sauce or wasabi unless you beg for it because each of Chef Miki's dishes arrives with its own perfectly paired sauce.

If you haven't made reservations in advance by several days, you may be waiting an hour or more on the sidewalk outside the restaurant (there is absolutely no room to stand and wait inside). To assuage that pain, try showing up early before the real crowd hits at around 6:30 p.m.

230 FOREST

230 Forest Ave., Laguna Beach, CA 92651
Reservations recommended: (949) 494-2545

Lunch & Dinner, average $12 – $30
Hours: Sun – Thurs, 11:00 a.m. – close
Corkage Fee: $15
Noise level at busiest: 9 out of 10
Good for kids? Not really
Dogs: No

Menu: www.LagunaBeachBest.com/Menus/230-Forest

While it's surprising to think of 230 Forest as a 19-year-old, it's not hard to believe that Executive Chef and Managing Partner Marc Cohen always finds a way to innovate the day-in, day-out menus, even 7,000 days later. He can't help himself. In fact, just a few weeks ago, Chef Marc rolled out an entirely new 230 Forest Menu for both lunch and dinner, changing up more than 60 percent of the existing menus.

In the process, he's re-invented sauces, dressings

and blends, and created layers of fresh vegetables, light pastas and grains. Take, for instance, his "refreshed" Chilean Sea Bass atop a sauté of fava beans, sweet corn and roasted mushrooms. The Sea Bass is dotted with a drizzle of saffron cream and Chef's own creation, tomato jam. It's a lovely blend of fresh, tastes.

For Chef Marc, his personal favorites are the Day Boat Scallops. He lines the just-caught scallops atop a perennial favorite, butternut squash risotto. He also prefers his Espresso Rubbed "1855" New York Strip Steak, with a rub concocted of espresso, chili and dry mustards and served with creamed spinach and (get this) blue cheese stuffed profiteroles.

He bustles off to his kitchen to create his own mini-menu for me. In minutes, he returns with a gorgeous Ceviche, tossed in a light mix of citrus juices and olive oil and served aboard taro root chips. Even while it's served like a mini tostada, the Ceviche's chip is flexible enough for folding, and it holds up sturdily under the juices and fresh fish.

Then, it's on to his Fried Brussels Sprouts & Bacon. Chef Marc and team cut pork loin squares and braise them in vinegar, apple juice, carrots, celery and clover honey for about three hours before quick-frying them with the Brussels Sprouts. Heaven.

Chef Marc surprises me with a refresh of one of my perennial 230 favorites, the Blackened Ahi Niçoise Salad. To date, his Niçoise Salad has always the finest in the land. I express concern about messing with perfection, but Chef Marc grins, trots away and eventually arrives with a dish that erases the very look of his former Salad from my memory banks.

A gorgeous lineup of the freshest Ahi tops greens, haricot vert, thin potato and egg slices, tomatoes and Kalamata olives. Capers skip across the Ahi tops, and just the slightest mustard vinaigrette drizzles the creation. Somehow, the best Niçoise Salad in the land has outdone itself.

With this refreshed menu, every taste on every dish stands apart as a unique entity ... and I suspect the same to be true for the remaining 42 items on the 230 Lunch and Dinner Menus.

SPLASHES

1555 S. Coast Highway, Laguna Beach, CA 92651
Reservations recommended: (888) 976-0820

Lunch & Dinner, average $16 – $36
Open for breakfast, lunch and weekend brunch. Dinner served Sun – Thurs 5:00 p.m. – 10:00 p.m.; Fri/Sat 5:00 p.m. – 11:00 p.m.
Corkage Fee: $20, limit one
Noise level at busiest: 3 out of 10
Good for kids? Workable
Dogs: No

Menu: www.LagunaBeachBest.com/Menus/Splashes-Restaurant

Some great chefs look like great chefs. And some great chefs look like regular, friendly dudes … on motorcycles.

David Fune is, understandably a great chef. The Executive Chef at *Surf and Sand Resort* for two years now, he oversees the majority of the culinary throughout the resort, and primarily lords over the decadent Splashes menu. In fact, Chef David has about 15 years in culinary at the highest levels in Southern California, including a gourmet food truck he drove to success with his cousin.

If he passed you on the street, though (especially while traveling on his Triumph motorcycle), you just wouldn't take the guy for a great chef at one of Laguna's renowned great resorts.

When he talks about food, motorcycles and his family, he is completely immersed and highly animated. This guy adores his three loves of life. But when he talks about food production at award-winning Splashes, it's all about his team and his genius Chef de Cuisine Julio Aguilar. Chef David is clearly the primary creator (or, at least, co-creator) of the revived menu since his coming on board, but there's not a lot of "I" in Chef David.

Most chefs just don't talk like that. Maybe this is why most chefs don't produce the kind of "foodie love" menu this guy does.

Adding Vibrancy to Every Plate

When Chef David came on board two years ago, he says one of the most significant changes had to do with color. "There was just too much brown on all the plates. I wanted to spark it up with really vibrant color, so that's where we started."

Now, every plate reflects the spark, with anything from flights of carrots (carrots done and plated three different ways) to bright tufts of micro greens and edible flowers.

"Most of our new dish creations actually start with the produce we want to work with, and then we build out from there," says Chef David. "It's just so important to have that freshness and color infused everywhere."

Then, it was about introducing different taste textures and taste sensations in each dish. Take, for instance, one of David's newest creations, his Ahi Marrow, so named because the pumpernickel lavash makes the dish look more like a bone marrow dish.

Rather than going with a normal lavash

flatbread (your usual tan cracker color), Chef wanted the deep color and crackle that pumpernickel would add, so he asked his bread supplier to create it for him.

"The pumpernickel holds up really well to the Ahi, both in flavor contrast and in that it doesn't get sogged down from the Ahi mix," says Chef. The mix itself is sushi grade Ahi, fried capers, spinach and ginger all piled into the slightly hollowed lavash. It's then topped with micro basil, white radish shavings and colorful edible flowers.

As Chef David predicts, it's a gorgeous taste treat with layers of flavors and crunch.

The Brussels Sprouts dish, with kudos to Chef de Cuisine Julio, proffers another example of a combined taste treat of sweet and savory in an Asian-influenced presentation. The Brussels are first fried in smoked Uzu curd, Uzu being an Asian fruit that sits somewhere between grapefruit and mandarin orange in flavor.

While the chefs could probably stop there with the "sweet and savory" equation already solved, they create a mellow soy sauce, add julienned black and white radish (for peppery bite), cilantro and Asian parsley, and toss it all together for a heavenly creamy/smoky/crisp sensation.

Given that fish and shellfish are usually the most popular items on this resort's menus, Chef offers a variety of options to please any palate.

For years, scallops at the Splashes resort had been served with risotto and, while Chef David has nothing against risotto, he wanted to change up the color and texture here, too. This time, Chef reached back to the Egyptian Pharaohs for their "forbidden rice," an aromatic black rice that was once reserved for royalty and buried with Pharaohs (because every Pharaoh needs his starch).

"Forbidden rice has this amazing nutty flavor but it can be a little chewy, so we actually overcook it on purpose to give it a creamy, soft texture," says Chef David.

Then, Chef takes a mirepoix of vegetables (a mix of chopped asparagus, onion and carrots), adds in super-crunchy kale, then purées the mix with milk and seasonings to create a flavorful sauce with a nice bit of crunch. Of course, now that I've fallen in love with my Scallops dish, Chef tells me he's changing it. This is the problem with chefs, heavy sigh. They're always coming up with something new.

He assures me, though, that the primary dishes he's introduced to me will, for the most part, remain the same. "We're just doing some seasonal updates with seasonal vegetables and sauces," he says.

In the end, the Splashes menu is as enticing as the setting the restaurant itself enjoys, nestled on the sand with its enormous glass doors flung open to the breeze. Finally, for this local, the culinary talent and taste has surpassed the extraordinary view.

At Press Time: Brussels Bistro: Surprising Haute Cuisine

222 Forest Ave., Laguna Beach, CA 92651
(949) 376-7955

Just as we were going to press, I wrote a dining review on the surprising Euro high-level cuisine by Chef Thomas at Brussels Bistro. Don't let this comfortable-looking pub fool you! This is mighty French and Belgian cuisine. See www.LagunaBeachBest.com and search "Brussels."

Best Casual Dining & Lunches

Lumberyard
384 Forest Ave. • Laguna Beach

Lumberyard

384 Forest Ave. • Laguna Beach

LUMBERYARD

384 Forest Ave., Laguna Beach, CA 92651
(949) 715-3900

Lunch average, $5 – $17
Hours: Mon – Friday, 11:30 a.m. – midnight,
Sat/Sun 11:00 a.m. – midnight
Noise level at busiest: 5 out of 10 in restaurant (without live music),
2 out of 10 on patio
Good for kids? Yes
Dogs? Allowed outside of patio

Menu: www.LagunaBeachBest.com/Menus/Lumberyard-Lunch

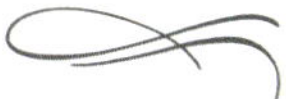

I probably eat at the Lumberyard more than any other restaurant in Laguna Beach because it's just so darn easy to get together there with friends. My BFF, Lisa, and I meet there at least once a month for lunch on

the patio as it's easy to bring her beloved dog (my god-dog), Bindi, along.

And, the Lumberyard is central with (usually) plentiful parking to meet local friends for happy hour. It's usually easy to grab a table, the wait staff is always friendly, and there are plenty of locals around to chat with.

Here's my blog take on the Lumberyard lunch menu:

The Lumberyard Laguna Beach is a dog-friendly venue. While they don't allow the dog to sit in the patio with you, they let the dog sit just on the other side of the short patio wall (in full view of you), and then attend quite heartily to said dog throughout your meal. In fact, last I heard, one of the waitresses who makes all the aprons for the Lumberyard staff says that she's making a custom bandana for Bindi. (Sorry, you must have lunch at the Lumberyard at least 28 times a year to qualify for a dog bandana.)

I'm convinced the Lumberyard serves up the finest Crabcake Salad in town. It's a hearty serving of greens, pear slices, fresh asparagus and two hot-off-the-griddle sizable crabcakes, all topped in bleu cheese. Criminy, it's fabulous.

Their roasted beet salad is quite good and, on the rare occasion that my buddy, Lisa, is having a bad day, they're happy to throw flash-fried calamari on her Caesar salad. (They'll throw just about anything you want on their salads; they're quite affable.)

The Lumberyard offers a $10 lunch menu, too, which now includes an Artichoke/Mushroom Panini that's every level of comfort and crunch you need. The menu also covers a number of salads, half sandwich combos, burgers, BBQ pulled pork and more.

... And since I'm mentioning burgers ... the Signature Lumberyard Burger is one fine specimen. (See my *Top Four Gourmet Burgers* review at www.LagunaBeachBest.com.) At this point, the Signature Lumberyard Burger offers a heck of a tall wall for other burgers to climb over.

While I'm focused on lighter fare lunch items here, note that the Lumberyard offers a great Cedar Plank Salmon, a serious Sea Bass entree, and five different (large ounce) steaks. And if you're having one of those really terrible horrible days, their Chicken Pot Pie will fix you right up ... and I daresay THAT'S the only Chicken Pot Pie you'll find in Laguna Beach.

I like the Lumberyard. It's casual, unpretentious and its serving staff is great. It's a comfort food place, even when you're plowing through the healthier items on the menu. It's a very decent lunchtime spot, dog or sans dog.

CAFÉ ANASTASIA

470 Ocean Ave., Laguna Beach, CA 92651
(949) 497-1212

Lunch, average: $10 – $13
Hours: 7 a.m. – 3 p.m.
Noise level at busiest: 2 out of 10 on patio, 4 out of 10 inside
Good for kids? It's OK but kids can get fidgety
Dogs: Yes on patio

Menu: www.LagunaBeachBest.com/Menus/Café-Anastasia-lunch

OK, perhaps I've belabored my point with my breakfast reviews of Cafe Anastasia. I think these folks serve the best breakfast in Laguna Beach, period. But, fact is, they also serve a mean lunch.

For starters, our Anastasia chefs don't know what "small portions" means. You'll be able to split just about any gargantuan serving if you can stand only eating one thing. But that IS the conundrum here.

The Anastasia sandwiches are spectacular, all running between $9 and $11. The Poulet with blackened chicken breast, avocado and smoked gouda is a best seller, as is its Italian take on a Caprese salad with basil, fresh tomatoes, buffalo mozzarella and pesto piled onto Ciabetta bread.

Their salads are fresh and very tasty – my favorites are the Salade Nicoise (seared tuna, greens, green beans, hard-boiled egg, potatoes, olives, etc.) and the divine Pasta Salad with Grilled Chicken (penne pasta in pesto with sun-dried tomatoes and roasted pine nuts). (Hey! That counts as salad, right? I mean, they CALL it a salad, right?)

If that's not enough to stuff you to the gills, Anastasia's has huge pasta dishes and thin crust pizzas to boot. Even their daily soups are delectable. I tell you, these people so rarely go wrong, I can't even remember the last time they were less than an "8" on a scale of 10 in my book.

Life in Laguna Beach

The bus bench in front of Laguna's Library.

AVILA'S EL RANCHITO

1305 S. Coast Highway, Laguna Beach, CA 92651
(949) 376-7040

Lunch, dinner average: $7 – $14
Hours: Mon – Fri, 11:00 a.m. – 9:00 p.m.;
Sat/Sun, 10:00 a.m. – 10:00 p.m.
Noise level at busiest: In the bar: 7 out of 10 (TVs are loud),
In the restaurant: 4 out of 10.
Good for kids? Yes
Dogs: Yes, on the outdoor patio

Menu: www.LagunaBeachBest.com/Menus/El-Ranchito-Laguna-Beach

A couple years ago, I realized that months were passing between visits with one of my good friends, Rhonda. So, we established a standing monthly "Soup Date" at Avila's El Ranchito in Laguna Beach to ensure we maintain contact in our busy lives.

There's just nothing better than Mama's Avila Soup, a giant bowl of their version of "chicken soup for the soul" with chicken, rice, avocado, cilantro, onions and tomatoes. It arrives steaming hot with a full set of warm tortillas. It's a soup I've ordered "to go" more than any other item in town, and it's the same soup I'd scoop up on my way home to thaw

my bones from a freezing outrigger practice. "We've had people call us and tell us that they're so sick they can't even come in to the restaurant to pick up their soup," says Michael Avila, grandson to founders Salvador and Margarita and owner of the Laguna Beach restaurant. "We tell them to just come down the alley behind the restaurant for a quick pass-off. They usually drive up in their pajamas, bless their hearts."

Comfort Food Mexi Style

The soup is a crowning comfort food, assuredly. And, if you think about it, that's what Avila's El Ranchito is really all about – comfort Mexican food. Every item, from the front-runner Guacamole Fresco on forward is a big heap of goodness and love, originated by now-90-year-old Grandma Margarita Avila.

Avila's El Ranchito enjoys 11 locations in Orange County, having first opened in Huntington Beach in 1966. Each restaurant is owned and operated by a family member with about 80% of the menu still featuring original items from Grandma Margarita. Each owner, based on his or her community's feedback and desires, completes the remaining 20% of the menu.

Michael first stepped into the ownership side of the business when he and his wife, Christine, helped his dad (Victor) open the San Clemente location. They began two days after returning from their honeymoon in 2003, and their dog, Hallie, immediately took up the greeter's position at the front stoop.

In 2006, Michael and Christine stepped into their own restaurant ownership in Laguna Beach.

"When we heard this restaurant space was open in Laguna Beach, we jumped right on it," says Michael. "Laguna Beach has such a cool, beach vibe. People who live here actually *go* to their own beach, and that makes for a lot of happy, relaxed people."

As restaurateurs go, Michael is pretty darned happy and relaxed, too. He greets newcomers and regulars as if you've been longtime buddies. There is a natural friendliness and graciousness here, and Michael talks about his family and Grandma's cooking with equal love and grace.

A couple weeks ago, about 30 of us went over to my Grandparents' house for my Grandfather's birthday," he says. "And Grandma's still in the kitchen, just like she's always been, showing us how to create this or that," says Michael.

"And I've got to tell you ... we all re-create her recipes to the letter, but there's just something about the love in her hands that makes her version better. She's been such an awesome model to follow."

Something For Every Comfort Need

The majority of the Laguna Beach El Ranchito menu (that 80%) comes compliments of Grandma Margarita, and it's an expansive collection of favorites. For starters, breakfast is served all day long at El Ranchito with *Huevos Rancheros* actually selling in greater number in the evening rather than morning hours. And, Happy Hour runs Monday through Friday, 3 p.m. – 6 p.m. all year long.

The margarita menu alone boasts more than 20 varieties, each of which is amenable to at least 30 tequila choices.

If it's lunch or dinner you're interested in, you might want to share a platter or two. My friend, Rhonda, and I shared Grandma's Chingolinga a stylish, flaky pastry filled with the restaurant's trademark slow-cooked chicken. It's sliced into portions and served with a hefty dose of rice and beans.

While a number of popular appetizers and salads grace the menu, our dear Grandma Avila created a number of large dish specialties including her own "Chimi-Changa," Blackened Calamari Tacos, Baja Bowls, sautéed shrimp and garlic in her Shrimp al Mojo de Ajo dish, Carne Asade, Chile Verde and Chicken in "Mama Avila's Mole Sauce."

The dear woman didn't stop there, however, as the menu goes on for another three pages with rellenos, tacos, tamalas, flautas, enchiladas, burritos and every kind of combination.

Give Them What They Want.

Although every Avila restaurant cheerily replicates these tried-and-true recipes, each owner has plenty of latitude to flex the existing dishes and create and customize new items to his or her own community. "The key to making people happy is simple," says Michael. "You give them what they want." "When people want to order breakfast items, we give them ALL the breakfast items to choose from. When they're vegetarians who are sick of eating salads, we came up with a great avocado burrito. When they're waiting in line and their kids are starving, we'll toss a quick cheese quesadilla together," says Michael. "It's just so easy to help people out," he says. "All you have to do is ask."

CARMELITA'S KITCHEN DE MEXICO

217 Broadway St., Laguna Beach, CA 92651
Reservations recommended: (949) 715-7829

Lunch/Dinner, average $8 – $19 Hours: 11:00 a.m – 11:00 p.m. except Sunday, 11:00 a.m. – 9:00 p.m.
Noise level at busiest: 9 out of 10
Good for kids? Yes
Dogs: No

Menu: www.LagunaBeachBest.com/Menus/Carmelitas-Laguna-Beach

In previous years, I can't say I've dined on anything very memorable in what we locals call the "food court" of Laguna Beach at the corner of PCH and Broadway. This space is usually reserved for standard beach fare cuisine for all those folks across the street on Main Beach. For years, it's produced nothing memorable.

It was a blessed event, then, to finally feast at Carmelita's. Their presence in the "food court" has created a complete transformation in foot traffic this coming summer.

Carmelita's is a small, family-owned chain with only three other locations. When Carmelita's won the bid for the old Crab Shack spot (beating out Chipotle), we waited anxiously until our anxiouses were sore. A full year later in mid-September 2012, they finally opened their doors. I remained skeptical, even while driving by on several occasions and noting the large number of patrons they seemed to be hauling in.

Finally, I stuck a toe in their door. With its rich woods and full wrap-around bar, Carmelita's is a far cry from anything that's occupied this space before. The place is impeccably clean and there is no shortage of great, friendly staff. The wait for its arrival in Laguna Beach was well worth it.

All of the margaritas at Carmelita's are basically "skinny" as Carmelita's only uses agave and fresh juices. My favorites are the Partida Margarita and the Basil & Cucumber Margarita. (See my Top Margaritas in Laguna Beach in the *Happy Hours* section for details.)

Carmelita's Menu: Highly Creative

Chips are homemade and crispy hot, served up with their "family recipe" black bean queso dip and a fresh salsa, and it's an unlimited supply. On my very first visit, my buddy and I spent a long time reviewing all the many options on the menu – it is extensive! First, the Enchiladas de Mariscos (dungeness crab, shrimp, avocado and cream topped with their fabulous chile verde sauce and a polite dab of whipped sour cream). And, after finally omitting the Lobster Chile Rellenos and the Pollo A La Chipotle from our list, we settled on Tacos de Hongos (ribeye steak on a bed of grilled portabella mushrooms with onion and cheese).

These were absolutely fabulous dishes, period. And ever since then, I've been coming back for more.

Photo credit: Diane Alms

At some point along the way, I stopped into Carmelita's and the floor manager squeezed me into a bar stool spot just a couple feet from the kitchen action. After seeing plate after plate delivered to the servers, I decided on the Villa Rica, a pan-seared sea bass with salsa verucizanna, vera cruz rice and spinach. Lightly charred on the outside, the chunk of sea bass that arrived was so flaky and tender it was a melt-in-your-mouth experience. I think both Eva's Caribbean and 230 Forest serve up a heck of a sea bass, but I'm here to tell you – Carmelita's might just have swiped the crown. The accompanying white rice mixed with seared corn had a lovely hint of mint, and the spinach tasted almost wood-smoked. The dish, as a whole, was amazing.

Given that I scarfed the entire plate of food down WITH one of their classic skinny margaritas, I had no room for dessert. If I DID have any room remaining, I'd go after the dessert they kept serving up on the line – a Treslechu Cake, which looked to be white chocolate cake with a strawberry/chocolate center and three seared campfire marshmallows on the side.

Still later on another visit, it was Carmelita's Tampiquerra I had to try – three marinated, seared planks of prime steak stacked atop a cheese enchilada in red sauce with handmade guacamole on the side. It was quite a tower to behold, and I'm glad I brought a friend along to share the plate. This was an insanely delicious dish.

I've probably visited Carmelita's 12 or so times, and not once have I been even mildly disappointed. My thanks to Camelita's for finally bringing lasting, foodie flavor to that little corner of our Laguna world. It's been a long time coming!

COYOTE GRILL

31621 S. Coast Highway, Laguna Beach, CA 92651
Reservations recommended: (949) 499-4033

Dinner, average $8 – $13
Hours: Breakfast 7 a.m. – noon; Sat/Sun 7 a.m. – 2 p.m.;
Lunch noon – 5 p.m.; Dinner 5 p.m. – 9 p.m.
Noise level at busiest: 9 out of 10
Good for kids? Yes
Dogs: No

Menu: www.LagunaBeachBest.com/Menus/Coyote-Grill

For years, I've lived about 30 yards from The Coyote Grill. Except for the early, weekday mornings when I might trot up for an early breakfast, Coyote is always basking in a happy jumble of noise. On weekends, the jumble becomes more of a boisterous uproar, particularly on summer afternoons. While the volume subsides as you move west to the restaurant's back patio, the place is jaunty. It's just a fun place to be, period. Even the bartenders and servers – many of whom have worked at Coyote Grill for 12, 18, even 25 years – are happy. "We've been family owned for so many years now that we've

'acquired' family members along the way," says Desirée Gomez, the General Manager. "It's not just the people who work for us. We have hundreds of regulars, and they've all become family, too." Indeed, walk in any time of the day or night, and you'll hear people greeting each other as if they haven't seen each other in years. Coyote Grill is, quite simply, one of Laguna Beach's iconic neighborhood bars.

Mexican Fare, Laguna Beach Flair

Day after day, Coyote serves up Baja-style Mexican breakfasts (including a rare Fish & Eggs dish), lunches, hefty happy hours and dinners. Daily, they make their own sweet-and-sour mix, fry their own tortilla chips and create 10 gallons of their salsa and salsa verde ("we dice every single one of those tomatoes," says Desirée). Coyote offers six different kinds of fresh fish on the daily menu, which includes Mahi-Mahi and Calamari in the popular fish tacos. And, from October to March, the Grill serves the most sublime Baja-style local grilled lobster you can get your hands on. Lastly, let's not forget the extensive Happy Hour Menu and the 100+ types of tequila you can request in drinks or shots.

All in the Family

Kim Bryant took over this particular restaurant space from longtime Cove restaurateurs in 1989. Prior, Bryant was an existing 9-year owner of Café Del Coyote in San Clemente (now the Pizza Port). Given that all four of his children grew up in his restaurants, it's no surprise that they've remained involved to this day.

While Desirée began working the front of the house at 12 years of age, older brother, Justin, started working in the kitchen, and younger brother, Jarrod, followed the same path. Eventually, little sister Tiana came on board, too, as a server. When Dad made his move to South Laguna Beach, the entire kid brood moved over to Coyote Grill, too. While the oldest, Justin, moved to Dad's ranch in Hawaii, the three remaining children single-handedly manage Coyote's daily business.

The locals have supported the family every step of the way. Strike up a conversation with any of the clientele here and they'll tell you how long they've been coming to Coyote Grill and what they religiously order. For me it's the Baja Grilled Lobster and the Crab Ceviche. By far these are two favorite staples of mine across Laguna Beach. Additional suggestions: Be sure you try the Coconut Shrimp, breakfast's Beef Machaca, the Jalapeno Bacon Wrapped Shrimp, and the classic Cove Fried Chicken, carried over on popular demand from 1978. Even the Americanized Coyote Burger is a work of art.

Event Watch

Go to the Calendar at LBBest.com for Fresh Local Lobster announcements from Coyote Grill.

EVA'S CARIBBEAN KITCHEN

31732 S. Coast Highway Laguna Beach, CA 92651
Reservations recommended: (949) 499-6311

Dinner average $14 – $30
Hours: Tuesday – Sunday 5:00 p.m. – close
Noise level at busiest: 4 out of 10
Good for kids? Yes
Dogs? No

Menu: www.LagunaBeachBest.com/Menus/Evas-Caribbean

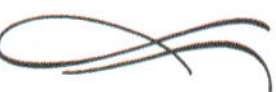

Eva serves up a classic Caribbean menu – it's the only one in Laguna Beach and, thankfully, it is a stellar one. A great cook in her own right, Eva didn't consider herself a cook at all when she first agreed to becoming a "silent" partner in the restaurant. In no time at all, though, she was calling up her mother and aunt for ideas, both of whom specialized in Caribbean and South American dishes. She eventually hired a new chef, and everything began to sync in a whole new way.

The collaboration has produced the finest around in Cornmeal Catfish, Creole Stew, Seared Chilean Sea Bass, jerk chicken and fish dishes, curry dishes, and blackened fish and steak dishes. Order your entreé selection with the level of spice you prefer, and enjoy a variety of inventive salsas and chutneys with each.

(Important note though: Before you even consider tackling the entrée items, you must try the Crab and Sweet Corn Cakes or the Conch Fritters aka: Caribbean Viagra.)

365 Bottles of Rum on the Wall ...

More importantly, ask Eva to help you pair your dinner selection with one of the restaurant's 365 rums, one of the most extensive and rarest collections of rums in North America. While she has created 16 rum-based cocktails, Eva also offers a variety of singles or flights, and she's happy to provide a bit of education on your selection if you so choose.

See my LagunaBeachBest.com/Calendar for Eva's popular Food & Rum Pairing Events. Hosted many times a year, she might do a Rum & Chocolate event, or a Rum & Cigars event ... she never runs out of ideas, and her lucky attendees never tire of the amazing rums she introduces.

The food is always great at Eva's, but the ambience itself rivals the unique menu. Locals here call it "The Eva Experience," and it definitely feels as if you've stepped into Eva's home dining room for cocktails and dinner as Eva is a fun, engaging host.

Don't expect to be in a rush here at Eva's. Signs will remind you that you're on Caribbean time, and they mean it. Relax, enjoy your rum, feast on your fabulous entreé and finish the evening with Eva's freshly made Coconut Crème Bruleé and strong South American coffee.

There were few better moments in Laguna Beach restaurant history when this "silent partner" stepped up as the welcoming force at the front door, and the operational brains in the kitchen. Eva's is an island experience worth savoring.

GINA'S PIZZA AND PASTARIA

3 locations:
610 N. Coast Highway, Laguna Beach, CA 92651, (949) 497-4421
1100 S. Coast Highway, Laguna Beach, CA 92651, (949) 494-4342
Summers during festival season: On the Pageant of the Masters Grounds

Lunch, Dinner, average $6 – $12
Sun – Thurs 11:00 a.m. – 9:00 p.m.; Fri/Sat 11:00 a.m. – 10:00 p.m.
Noise level at busiest: 4 out of 10
Good for kids? Yes
Dogs: Allowed on patios

Menu: www.LagunaBeachBest.com/Menus/Ginas-Pizza-Laguna-Beach

The other night, my lovely and affable niece, Karley, had to cancel Gina's Pizza plans, which caused great gnashing of teeth on both sides. We love Gina's Pizza.

I was so ready for Gina's Pizza, in fact, that I finally folded, called them and ordered a small pizza to go. Once your heart's set on Gina's, even steak and lobster pales in comparison.

Yes, they offer all the basic and popular combos. Yes, they allow you to create your own pizza. Yes, they have great antipastos, salads and quite phenomenal pastas and sandwiches. They even have wings. And, though I've taste-tested at least 15 dishes at this place, and though they really do have great food all around, I'll say for the second time — Gina's Pizza rocks.

There are other perfectly fine Italian restaurants in town, and I happen to love our recent newcomer, Pizza Lounge for thin-crust gourmet creations. Gina's just seems to have more of that old-fashioned-heaping-toppings-just-enough-grease that keeps everyone coming back for more.

Maybe it's the crust ... or crusts, as you can order their famous "traditional," or assuage your guilt with a whole grain or thin crust. (Fat lot it's going to do you with these toppings.)

Maybe it's the beachy atmosphere. Gina's has six locations in Orange County, but three of them are here in Laguna Beach right where Mama Gina began turning out pizzas in the 1950s. My favorite stop is on PCH and the corner of Oak – right in the middle of Laguna Beach – because you have the option to sit outside on the long, bar-stooled patio and watch all the people go by. It also seems to be a primary hangout for surfers, skimboarders and all-around groms, so pre-teen and teen girls always enjoy my recommendation for this location.

Maybe it's the fact that everyone working at any location I've been in seems to be having a good time there. In fact, even their delivery drivers are cool.

Whatever your excuse for Gina's, just make sure you get in there. You can thank me later after you waddle your way home.

LAGUNA COFFEE COMPANY

1050 S. Coast Highway, Laguna Beach, CA 92651
949-494-6901

Average: $7 – $9
Hours: Mon – Wed, 6 a.m. – 6 p.m.; Thurs & Fri, 6 a.m. – 8 p.m.; Sat 6:30 a.m. – 8 p.m., Sun, 7 a.m. – 6 p.m.
Noise level at busiest: 1 out of 10 on patio, 5 out of 10 inside
Good for kids? Yes
Dogs: Yes
Wi-Fi: Yes

Menu: www.LagunaBeachBest.com/Menus/Laguna-Coffee

When our French chef, Sylvan, owned and ran Laguna Coffee, he introduced a tantalizing menu of pastries, cookies and European-style paninis.

Thankfully, when the Ackleys took over in ownership, they kept Sylvan involved in the heart of the business. While he still trots in to bake and

cook up various batches of great food, he's also meticulously trained a few of the staffers to reproduce his gems.

For a hearty lunch sandwich, there's no better than Sylvan's Panini. Order from a menu of 6 Panini offerings ...

- Simple 3-Cheese Grilled
- Croque Monsieur (Black Forest ham, Swiss cheese and tomatoes)
- Florentine (pictured here with turkey, Provolone and Parmesan cheese and spinach)
- Portofino (turkey, Provolone cheese, tomatoes and basil)
- Primavera (vegetarian with artichoke hearts, roasted peppers, spinach, tomato, basil and Provolone cheese), or
- "Dennis' Special" (you just have to ask on this one!)

Whatever your choice, and whatever your bread selection, five minutes will see your Panini delivered in all its hearty, steamy gloriousness.

At Press Time: Laguna Coffee Expands to Wines & Beers With Cheese & Meat Platters

Just as this book was going to press, we learned that Laguna Coffee had expanded its hours and menus once again. Now, get your coffee fix in the morning, and return in the afternoon and evening for wine, beers and cheese platter munchies! The team has also expanded its live music repertoire to accompany your happy hour mode.

Go to www.LagunaBeachBest.com and search for "Laguna Coffee" in the search function to read all the newest menu details.

photo credit: Laguna Coffee Co.

LA SIRENA GRILL

2 locations:
347 Mermaid St., Laguna Beach, CA 92651 (949) 497-8226
30862 S. Coast Highway, Laguna Beach, CA 92651 (949) 499-2301

Breakfast/Lunch/Dinner average, $4 – $12
Hours: Every day, 8 a.m. – 10 p.m.
Noise level at busiest: 2 out of 10 in restaurant
Good for kids? Yes
Dogs? Yes, on patios

Menu: www.LagunaBeachBest.com/Menus/La-Sirena-Grill

La Sirena is a very tasty little Mexican restaurant with a heart and mind for conservation. The restaurant only serves organic food, and aims to create "zero waste" in its efforts.

First established in a tiny love shack on Mermaid Street in downtown Laguna Beach, La Sirena serves long lines of faithful followers morning,

noon and night. The restaurant expanded to a second location in South Laguna Beach in the Haggen's shopping center a few years ago, and then tripled its space again there in 2012 to include a long bar with a massive assortment of beers and tequilas.

After years in the kitchen and front of the house, Jeff Elias took over the "beer program," and the man is one accomplished Tap Meister. He produces pie charts of beer flavor wheels to educate his staff, and has gained something of a reputation of matchless pairings between certain beers and the La Sirena food.

No matter which La Sirena you choose, you're going to have very authentic Mexican food with a unique gourmet touch. Try the Blackened Wild Salmon Tacos, the Calamari (giant) Burritos or the top-selling Sirena Plate, which consists of a Grilled Pasilla Chile stuffed with herb cheese, herb-marinated bell peppers, onions and freshly made spicy pico de gallo. Their Blackened Wild Salmon Salad is also a favorite of mine. Kids have their own menus, too.

At Press Time: The Four Best Hamburgers in Laguna Beach

After extensive research, I narrowed in on the Four Top Gourmet Burgers in Laguna Beach (gourmet meaning that they appear on menus where you wouldn't commonly expect to see a burger).

The article is too entirely long for this book, but you can quench your curiosity by going to www.LagunaBeachBest.com and searching "hamburgers" to see if you agree with me.

MANDARIN KING RESTAURANT

1223 N. Coast Highway, Laguna Beach, CA 92651,
(949) 494-8992 for reservations or take-out

Breakfast/Lunch/Dinner average, $8 – $15
Hours: Monday – Thursday, 11:30 a.m. – 9:30 p.m.; Friday, 11:30 a.m. – 10:00 p.m., Saturday, noon – 10:00 p.m.; Sunday, 3:00 p.m. – 9:00 p.m.
Noise level at busiest: 3 out of 10
Good for kids? Yes
Dogs? No

Menu: www.LagunaBeachBest.com/Menus/Mandarin-King

It's no surprise that people continue to crowd their way to Mandarin King. Step foot in the 30-year old operation of Mandarin King and you feel special. Mandarin King knows how to throw down a serious Chinese food experience, too.

With more than 65 main dishes on the menu and added soups, rices and salads, it seems there's easily something for everyone, but Aaron assures me that every dish is easily customized.

"You could say we're Traditional American Chinese," says Aaron. "We're 'traditional' to the point of introducing great Asian vegetables like Chinese mustard greens and age-old spices, but we're 'American' in that we custom create every order according to what a person wants.

A Family Serving Families

Mandarin King is only closed four days of the year – Easter, July 4th, Thanksgiving and Superbowl. Chef Tan has worked the other 361 days of the year for more than 20 years here at Mandarin King. Chef Gui has done the same for nearly 15 years.

"We grew up calling all the staff here 'aunt' and 'uncle' because they've all been family to us, too," says Aaron.

With their mission statement focused on "tradition, community and family," Mandarin King continues to provide family-style dining at every table. While guests can freely share their over-large portions with friends and family, they can order food any ol' way they want – gluten free, low sodium, low oil, less vegetables, more vegetables, vegetarian, vegan and ... of course ... never any MSG.

As he chats, Mom Priscilla arrives with Cream Cheese Wontons, one of their tried-and-true best sellers on the appetizer menu.

From there, it's a pile-on of food. Aaron confesses to loving the Honey Walnut Shrimp dish as a kid long before it arrived on the menu.

This dish is spectacularly rich and coddling. The shrimp is flash fried, then stir fired with cream sauce made of mayonnaise, coconut milk, lemon and spices. It's finished with candied walnuts and sides of broccoli and carrots.

"There aren't a lot of mayonnaise based recipes in Asia," say Aaron. "But, we're Traditional *American*, and it sure tastes great in this recipe."

I surface from my Honey Walnut Shrimp daze to Mongolian Beef and King Pao Chicken, another two best selling dishes at Mandarin. The Mongolian Beef is simply sauced and stir-fried with green and white onions. The beef is very tender and flavorful, whisper thin in its slices.

Where the Mongolian Beef is sublime, the Kung Pao Chicken is a robust pile of white chicken, peanuts, water chestnuts, ginger, green onions and plenty of red chili peppers tucked here and there.

While I didn't have the opportunity at this last visit, Aaron says the Spicy Peppered Fish is a great seller as well. The team serves up file of sole with fluffy breading, then stir fries with green peppers, jalapeno, onions and white pepper and an in-house secret sauce soy on the side.

With a bright New Year dawning, the Fu family assures me that they're going to be here many years ... 361 days each year. "None of us is going anywhere for a long time," says Aaron. "We're in it to end it – all together as a team, as a family – for our extended family."

MOZAMBIQUE STEAKHOUSE & COASTAL LOUNGE

1740 S. Coast Highway, Laguna Beach, CA 92651
Reservations: (949) 715-7777

Dinner average: $20 – $45
Hours: Mon – Thurs, 11 a.m. – 11 p.m.; Fri & Sat, 11 a.m. – midnight; Sunday, 11 a.m. – 11 p.m. Veranda Rooftop Lounge hours are 11 a.m. – sundown. Closed Christmas Day
Corkage fee: $20, 2 bottle maximum
Noise level at busiest: 3 out of 10
Good for kids? Yes, better on patios
Dogs? Allowed on downstairs Garden Patio and Veranda-Rooftop

Menu: www.LagunaBeachBest.com/Menus/Mozambique-Restaurant

When the Mozambique Steakhouse & Coastal Lounge set up shop in an enormous failed restaurant space at the corner of Agate and Coast Highway, we residents figured we'd be counting the days of its short existence, too.

photo credit: Mozambique Steakhouse

But, despite lagging and up-and-down economies and nearby neighborly concerns over parking and live music noise,

Mozambique has not only endured, but flourished. (Even better, the restaurant has actually befriended the neighbors, which is no small feat.)

Owners Ivan Spiers and George Poulus have not only created a lavish dining experience on three separate restaurant levels, but have earned a great reputation in town for their wholehearted help with various non-profit organizations in the city's limits. Additionally, they've created what is probably the most consistently "hot" live music venue in its second-floor lounge with international and popular regional bands gracing the stage several nights a week (see my review, *Happy Hours*).

Spawned from a boyhood love of South African tropical fruits and Peri-Peri spice, Mozambique's many dishes find a way to reflect those South African roots. (per Co-Owner George, the Peri-Peri is a mix of Birdseye pepper in a citrus/tomato base. Per my take, it's a spicy, complex wonder.)

When I say "many dishes" I mean just that – the Mozambique Dinner Menu reads like a multi-page novel.

Mozambique's Dinner menu is by far the most generous offering of assorted meats, fish and vegetarian dishes in Laguna Beach. (Then, of course, you also have large Lunch, Happy Hour and Sunday Brunch menus to choose from, too.)

Your most difficult task comes from choosing between more than 20 appetizers, soups and salads, 20 "Mozambique signature favorites," and 12 hearty menu items on the Steakhouse Grill side of the menu. Many of these items are also offered in smaller portions for lighter appetites, but I prefer to order the full meal and happily trot home with a "to go" box under my arm – the food is worthy of a second visit the next day!

Even after all these years, I've only skimmed the surface of the immense Mozambique menu. I love the Peri-Peri Prawns ... the Seared Tuna Steak with its shoyu mustard beurre blanc ... the Filet Mignon with mashed potatoes and asparagus ... and the to-die-for New Zealand Lamb Chops with saffron couscous and ratatouille sides. And, when the mood strikes, I can safely say that there's no better Fish 'n Chips in Laguna than what you'll find at Mozambique.

(And while we're on the subject of "mood striking," be sure to dive into the Mozambique dessert menu, too. Aside from items like the flourless chocolate ganache and chocolate and banana bread pudding, you simply must try the Portuguese Hot Butter Pudding. Good glory.)

At Press Time: NeaPolitan Pizza Has New Ownership, Greatly Improved Food

31542 S. Coast Highway, Laguna Beach, CA 92651
(949) 499-4531

We weren't able to interfere in this book's press run to insert my entire new review on the revamped NeaPolitan Pizza in South Laguna Beach.

Their experienced take on running a first-class pizzeria – and all the many pasta and fish dishes they are installing now – is worth the read at LagunaBeachBest.com ... just search for "Nea" in the search function.

NICK'S

440 S. Coast Highway, Laguna Beach, CA 92651
(949) 376-8595

Breakfast, Lunch & Dinner, average Breakfast $7 – $12,
Lunch and Dinner, $12 – $26
Hours: Breakfast weekends only, 7:30 a.m. – 11:30 a.m.,
Lunch/Dinner, 11:00 a.m. – close.
Noise level at busiest: 7 out of 10
Good for kids? Yes
Dogs: No

Menu: www.LagunaBeachBest.com/Menus/Nicks-Laguna-Beach

Nick's comes from the same genetic lines of The Claim Jumper, so let's just state one fact going in: You're going to get a heap of food.

When every other restaurant begins to sweep up and stack chairs at night, Nick's is still rocking. This is a cool, urban-styled restaurant right smack in the middle of all the action on PCH. In 2008, it took over the old (long-time) Cabana Grill space and changed things up significantly with a sleek, large bar, exposed brick and dark woods, and a small patio that peeks to the ocean and provides great people watching.

I remember the first week Nick's opened, my BFF, Lisa, and I visited. After perusing the menu, she told the manager, "You're not going to make it here with this much fried food." (I thought that was terribly ballsy of her, but she did have a point.) I'm not sure that they took her at her word (given her history in Laguna Beach, I'd definitely listen to the girl), but they have morphed the menu to more fresh foods and fish dishes over time.

Granted, Nicks still offers its best-selling breaded Asparagus Fries and Fried Deviled Eggs, but it also offers yummy Blackened Sea Bass Tacos and Ahi Tartare in the appetizers section, too.

Nick's Sandwiches are ginormous. They stand something like 6 inches tall and measure the circumference of the alien spaceships captured at Area 51. The Blackened Halibut Sandwich and the Ribeye Melt are simply killer. I hear their Reuben is the best (and sloppiest) in Laguna Beach, and their two burger offerings are about the size of Texas.

For me, I like the hearty Grilled Steakhouse Salad, and the Warm Potato Salad is something you have to order on the side just to experience it once in your lifetime. (When I have large parties at my house, I order it by the gallon. It's not of this earth.)

Nick's offers a good series of fish (Sea Bass, Salmon, Cioppino) along with best sellers Fried Chicken, Meatloaf and Baby Back Ribs. We're talking comfort foods here, folks, and don't be apologizing for sitting down and scarfing it up.

ORANGE INN

703 S. Coast Highway, Laguna Beach, CA 92651
(949) 494-6085

Lunch average (and dinner in summer): $8 – $14
Hours: 6 a.m. to 5 p.m., June thru September, 6 a.m. to 9 p.m.
Noise level at busiest: 3 out of 10
Good for kids? Yes
Dogs: Yes

Menu: www.LagunaBeachBest.com/Menus/Orange-Inn

The last two weeks have been busy with friends dropping in from colder climes to soak up our Laguna Beach sunshine.

Being the Laguna Beach tour guide that I am, I've been trotting these friends to a variety of Laguna Beach restaurants.

When one of my visitors asked for a good old-fashioned sandwich, I was temporarily at a loss. I've tried plenty of hamburgers and veggie burgers in Laguna Beach (K'ya, Nicks, Belgian Bistro and Lumberyard Restaurant all scoring highly), and I have a couple favorite paninis, but it took some polling of fellow Laguna residents to land on a couple shops that provide significant fare in sandwiches.

As you know, I only mention the "best of," and I will say we visited four different restaurants that turned out sandwiches. For basic, meat-oriented sandwiches, my visitor's vote coincided with mine – Laguna Beach's Orange Inn. In the past, I've written about the Orange Inn one-of-a-kind coffee and breakfast (see *Breakfasts*), which creates snaking lines of customers out the quaint cottage's doors. Owner John Bodrero recently made a number of changes at the Orange Inn, though, and his expanded lunch menu adds well to his already popular sandwich board.

Maybe it's the sprouts that makes the Orange Inn sandwiches so memorable. Nearly every sandwich comes loaded with fresh, crunchy sprouts, lettuce and tomato, and the stack is a nice, hearty presentation. Or, maybe it's the fact that he doesn't load you down with overbearing bread rolls – most of the Orange Inn sandwiches are on bread slices like your Mom used to slap together for your school lunch bags. For me, I'd rather taste the filling inside than have to deal with a bunch of chewy bread.

We tried the Orange Inn's classic turkey avocado sandwich, the Albacore tuna sandwich, and John's new grilled chicken burger, all of which were freshly made and enjoyable entrees.

Happily, the grilled chicken burger was stellar (it arrived on a bun). I've gone back for this specific entry a number of times, and it's actually something I think about every time I drive by the darned place now. I can't say that many restaurants in Laguna Beach serve up a classic, old fashioned grilled chicken burger, but the Orange Inn has filled that gap nicely with two different grilled chicken options.

Eat inside in the cool surfer shack of the Orange Inn, or ask to take your sandwiches to go for a quick picnic just steps away at the beach.

PIZZA LOUNGE

397 S. Coast Highway Laguna Beach, CA 92651
(949) 497-2277 (takeout available)

Lunch, dinner average: $7 – 20
11:00 a.m. – 9:00 p.m.
Noise level at busiest: 5 out of 10
Good for kids? Yes
Dogs: No

Menu: www.LagunaBeachBest.com/Menus/Pizza-Lounge

A few weeks ago, a fellow Laguna Beach foodie recommended I try his vote for Laguna Beach's "best pizza," and, honestly, I was a little surprised.

Unfair as it might seem, when there are so many amazing restaurants in Laguna Beach, the residents here (me included) tend to gravitate away from the smaller "fast food" shops crowded around Main Beach. These little food joints have, historically, been "tourist staple fare" that run absolutely flat on the flair. I had assumed (quite wrongly) that the new Laguna Beach Pizza Lounge – on PCH just down from the Hotel Laguna –

was one such establishment.

Despite my protestations (not to mention my deep-seated, abiding love for Gina's thick-crust pizza), my foodie friend insisted I hoof it down to Gary Decker's Pizza Lounge … and my curiosity got the better of me. I took one of my girlfriends with me to assure complete objectivity.

Pizza Lounge's pizza by the slice …

Gary opened this little corner pizza restaurant in Laguna Beach in 2010 after experiencing great success creating these same pizza restaurants in Dallas. Although Pizza Lounge serves up hearty, grab-and-go slices from about 8 different daily pizza selections, these slices are the farthest thing from fast-food pizza imaginable.

For starters, the Pizza Lounge's two best sellers by the slice are not pepperoni … nope, they are:

- Artichoke-Pesto with Chicken
- Roasted Chicken with Goat Cheese and Olives
- California with Pepperoni, Bacon, Tomato, Spinach and Mozzarella
- You CAN ask for a simple pepperoni slice, but most patrons prefer to try the Pepperoni-Spinach-Bacon-Sliced Roma Tomato combo, instead (my choice, and I was very happily pleased).

And, one of Gary's latest creations – Coconut Shrimp Pizza – is quickly edging in as a 4th place contender for the shop's best selling slices. These pizzas are built on super thin, daily-crafted crusts, as Gary believes in piling on the flavors with just an "accent" of crust to "keep it all together." Pizza Lounge also creates gluten-free pizza, and has also introduced soy cheese as an option.

Pizza Lounge's pizzas in the round …

Beyond the obvious need to funnel great pizza by the slice to our wandering walk-about folks, Laguna Beach's Pizza Lounge also offers a huge menu of actual pizza (small, medium and extra large) for dine-in, take-out, and delivery. Choose from classics (cheese only, sausage/

pepperoni, Hawaiian, etc.), or try your hand at their best-selling gourmet entrees:

- Crowd favorite White Pizza with chicken and sausage,
- Pear and Gorgonzola Pizza,
- Santa Fe Taco Pizza,
- Veggie Light and Healthy Pizza or
- Basil Chicken and Pesto Pizza, just to name a few.

Not in the mood for pizza? Try a gargantuan salad (Pizza Lounge offers 14 varieties, which is quite probably the largest salad menu in all of Laguna Beach), grilled panini sandwiches and authentic falafels. My friend, Rhonda, and I split the Pear and Gorgonzola Salad and still couldn't nibble through its entirety.

To our dear proprietor, Gary Decker, my apologies for my wrong assumptions. Pizza Lounge is the phenomenal, thin-crust gourmet pizza experience we've all been waiting for in Laguna Beach. Well done!

At Press Time: Gary's Wife Is In on the Game, Too!

Ivory Restaurant
853 Laguna Canyon Rd. Laguna Beach, CA 92651
(949) 715-0261

While Gary Decker continues to expand his Pizza Lounge presence in various cities, his wife, Marsha Benson, has stepped into the restaurant business in Laguna Beach, too.

While Gary is involved in this venture, Marsha is the primary of this new eatery, Ivory Restaurant, which is next to the Sawdust Art Festival and adjacent to the old Laguna Culinary Arts school. See my review on this restaurant at www.LagunaBeachBest.com

ROOFTOP

1289 S. Coast Highway (top of La Casa del Camino),
Laguna Beach, CA 92651
Reservations only taken for parties of 6 or more: (949) 497-2446

Breakfast, lunch, average $9 – $15
Hours: Breakfast Saturday and Sunday ONLY, 9 a.m. – 11:30 a.m.,
Lunch 11:30 a.m. – 2:30 p.m.,
Noise level at busiest: 6 out of 10
Good for kids? Yes
Dogs: Yes

Menu: www.LagunaBeachBest.com/Rooftop-Laguna-Beach

This last week, my best friend, Lisa, and I stopped in for a quick lunch at the Rooftop.

Best ocean show in town

The Rooftop's lunch menu is provided by what I consider one of the best "foodie" restaurants in town, K'ya, which sits at the lobby level of the same hotel. Craig Connole, a Co-Owner and Master Chef of both locations, had to work hard to come up with menu items that could survive the trip up the many flights of stairs to Rooftop diners. He started with a small bar menu, and then expanded to what is now an impressive lunch menu.

What's for lunch?

The Rooftop offers 14 appetizers, from Chef Craig's famous Hawaiian Ahi Poke to Chicken Empanadas (we never pass these up), Guava BBQ Meatballs, a Charcuterie Platter and Cheese Fondue, to name a few.

The Rooftop's salads are offered in large and half sizes. My friend, Lisa, prefers the Grilled Ahi Nicoise, while I tend toward the Grilled Chicken Cobb (this is the best Cobb salad I've ever had anywhere).

Rooftop lunch entrees range from pasta dishes (try the Lobster Ravioli) to Hibachi Salmon (one of Craig's all-time best sellers in both restaurants) and Spicy Seafood Chowder. And, if that's not enough, the Rooftop offers "Petite" (allow me a brief moment to chortle here) Sandwich Platters. Choose a MONSTROUS sandwich of Blackened Chicken, Seared Ahi, Albacore Tuna, Shrimp Club, or Beef/Veggie burgers and then choose your sides and salads to accompany.

Well-trained dogs are allowed at the Rooftop Lounge, even including my best friend's gangling Bindi. Remember, your four-legged friend will have to trudge up a substantial number of stairs to get there, but dogs are treated well with their own water bowls upon arrival.

Don't forget that the Rooftop also serves Breakfast on weekends, too.

SLAPFISH RESTAURANT

211 Broadway Place, Laguna Beach, CA 92651
(949) 715-0464

Breakfast, lunch, average $6 – $18
Hours: Sun – Wed, noon to 8 p.m., Thur, Fri & Sat, 11 a.m. – 9 p.m.
Lunch 11:30 a.m. – 2:30 p.m.,
Noise level at busiest: 2 out of 10 (outdoor patio dining)
Good for kids? Yes
Dogs: Yes

Menu: www.LagunaBeachBest.com/Rooftop-Laguna-Beach

The Laguna Slapfish Restaurant is a smaller version of Chef Andrew Gruel's larger restaurant in Huntington Beach, but it's certainly not smaller in taste. With just a couple counter stools inside and a scatter of courtyard tables outside the restaurant, you could grab anything on the menu and be one seriously happy camper. Simply put, Slapfish is to fish and chips what Sprinkles is to cupcakes.

photo credit: Slapfish Restaurant

It all starts with the freshest possible sustainable fish, with a big emphasis on "sustainable." In fact, Chef Andrew's initial career path was only about sustainability of fish. Even as he ended up at the Aquarium of the Pacific to create educative programs that focused on seafood sustainability, he had no plan in his head to ever create a restaurant concept around sustainability.

"It just dawned on me one day that the most responsible way to live the sustainability message would be to actually create a hip food movement that only served sustainable fish and seafood," says Gruel.

And thus, in 2011, the Slapfish Food Truck was born. Sure enough, it proved a very successful "food movement" with fans flocking to Chef's food truck wherever it rolled. Now, he has six restaurants in play, from coast to coast, with more in the works.

Delectable Beach Fare Food

In keeping with its "grab and go" concept, the Slapfish Laguna restaurant is more focused on offering handheld food items and "food you can pick up with your fingers," says Chef.

On my visit, Chef Andrew slapped down hefty servings of his best-selling Fish Taco, Chowder Fries and Lobster Roll. Then, he had me try sides of the Lobster Dip 'n Chips and the Fried Pickles (which I have a profound weakness for).

The Fried Pickles were a mighty jumble, perfectly battered and served up with pickled red onion slices. The Lobster Dip was loaded with chunks of fresh lobster with a pile of house-made chips. And, the Fish Taco was piping hot,

crunchy, and drizzled in just enough Slapfish secret recipe chile sauce.

As it turns out, the Chowder Fries were a sudden invention back in the day when the Food Truck was running out of its Clam Chowder. To accommodate frenzied fans, the chefs doled out chowder on a pile of fries, and then topped the fries with their usual chowder toppings of bacon, chopped onion and cheese. Voila, an instant best seller was born.

The Lobster Roll, though – now this is the classic piece de resistance. Done "East Coast style," it's a split top large butter roll packed to the brim and beyond with big chunks of lobster tossed in a light, creamy dressing. It's ungodly it's so good.

I think our Laguna Beach food court has finally found its sustainable match.

Sushi Laguna

SUSHI LAGUNA

231 Ocean Ave., Laguna Beach, CA 92651
(949) 376-8786

Lunch/Dinner average $8 – $16
Hours: Noon – 9:30 p.m. daily
Noise level at busiest: 6 out of 10
Good for kids? Yes
Dogs: Yes

Menu: www.LagunaBeachBest.com/Sushi-Laguna

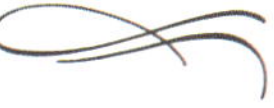

About 14 years ago, my first friend in Laguna Beach, Lisa, took me to lunch at Sushi Laguna on Ocean Avenue. On her recommendation, the "Monkey Balls" was my very first order. I have not been the same person since.

Now, granted, Monkey Balls are one of the baked items Owner and Chef Jay Sada has devised, but his sushi, sashimi and endless number of rolls are just as memorable.

The First Rule of sushi? Freshness. This is why I've been a tried and true fan of Sushi Laguna all these years. After testing at least 50 creations from

Owner and Sushi Chef Jay Sada, I have to say I can't remember a bite that was even slightly south of perfect freshness.

The Land of Opportunity

Raised in Fukuoka, Japan, Chef Sada learned the art of sushi chef at the age of 16. Years later, and on the suggestion of a good friend, he decided to pursue "greater opportunity" in the United States, and emigrated here at the age of 21.

He arrived with one acquaintance in L.A., and no English skills whatsoever. The friend dialed Chef Sada into a boarding house, and Sada purchased a television to help learn English.

"I knew absolutely NO English. My friend came over one night and wanted to go out for dinner, and I said, 'I'm studying English on the TV,' says Chef Sada. "And my buddy cracked up and said, 'But you're watching a Spanish program.' "

Initially working as a sushi chef in Seal Beach, Chef Sada moved around O.C. and even into Aspen, all the while looking for a restaurant in Orange County to call his own. The Ocean Avenue space opened in 2001, and Sushi Laguna was born that autumn. His was the fifth sushi restaurant in Laguna.

Even in the height of the summer season, at least 80% of Chef's crowd is made up of die-hard regulars, and they file to their favorite seats like

obedient children in a classroom. This is a friendly, boisterous place and the energy is contagious. Happily, the food is just as energetic.

The dining menu is packed with an amazing number of options for people not interested in raw fish ... 10 salads, 3 miso soups and 8 noodle soups, 8 vegetable dishes, 23 seafood dishes, 10 chicken and beef dishes ... the list goes on.

It's a happy meld of regions and spices and, while the dining menu is clearly overshadowed by the sushi preparations, it takes no backseat in flavor. Take, for instance, the Negimake Beef dish, a popular rib eye wrap coddling grilled scallions and asparagus served with a garlic teriyaki sauce. Or, try my favorite "cooked" dish, the Monkey Balls – deep fried spicy tuna serving as the stuffing in mushrooms.

Then, turn your attention to Sushi Laguna's 65 rolls. Or, try tackling the long sheet of sushi, sashimi and hand roll options with your little golf putt-putt pencil.

As far as Sushi Laguna's endless list of rolls goes, my go-to favorite has always been the Maui Roll (panko fried onion and avocado roll topped with Cajun tuna and jalapeno sauce) and the Salmon Lemon Roll (vegetables rolled and topped with fresh salmon and a thin slice of lemon with ponzu sauce).

I suggested that Chef come up with just one sushi item that's one of his favorites. He delivered Thai Sushi, a creation of raw shrimp topped in a simple lemon juice, a couple secret spices and sea salt. It was delicate and super flavorful, and is now on my permanent menu.

"The rice has to be fresh, too," says Chef Sada. "It's a combination of the two that makes the sushi something that people come back for."

Obviously, at Sushi Laguna it's a combination of something a little bit more.

THE DECK ON LAGUNA BEACH

627 Sleepy Hollow Lane, Laguna Beach, CA 92651
(949) 494-6700

Lunch/Dinner average $12 – $26
Hours: 11:00 a.m. – 10:00 p.m. daily
Noise level at busiest: 4 out of 10
Good for kids? Yes
Dogs: No

Menu: www.LagunaBeachBest.com/The-Deck

When I published the first edition of this book, I didn't include The Deck restaurant. Even though it has offered one of the coolest beachside vantage points on the Southern California coast, it had – with previous ownership – suffered with less-than-exciting food and service.

But that all changed in early 2013 when Chef Rainer Schwarz and his team took over as owners. Extensive renovations took place that Spring, which included the creation of The Deck's own kitchen (food was previously prepared in the former Beach House kitchen and trekked down flights of stairs to diners).

"It doesn't matter how good your food is," says Chef Rainer. "If you have to transport it a long way to get it to your diners, you're already in trouble. So, putting a kitchen in just for The Deck was the first and most important step."

Chef Rainer and his team of culinary wizards moved fully into play in June, 2013. Happily, The Deck on Laguna Beach has never been the same since.

Shouldered between The Pacific Edge Hotel and its popular bungalows and, on the other side, Chef's new Driftwood Kitchen (see page 41), the Deck enjoys a fantastic, reverberating vibe. Yes, the view is still amazing, but Chef's menu elevates the experience to a whole new game of play.

For Starters

At The Deck, Chef Rainer likes to keep the menu simple, offering between 10-12 small plates and another 10-12 entrées, with more frequent "change ups" occurring on the entire menu every two to three months.

Even the perennial items such as oysters change per the season. Diners can choose from three oyster offerings, and mix and match whatever they desire for their plate.

And More From the Sea

Chef de Cuisine Jesse Bajana trots out to explain the next dish – one of his favorites, The Deck Tacos. He is absolutely effervescent; he is so passionate about his food. "We have this awesome chorizo, so we basically melt it in a pan and then baste the Mexican white shrimp," he says with a cheery smile that you can't help smiling in return to.

He explains that the avocado salsa verde comes compliments of initially wolfing down street tacos on Olvera Street in L.A. "I love how they used

coriander and scallions to really perk up their salsa verde, so I adapted that taste, added a few other spices and just fold in the avocado ... and we end up with a fun signature dish."

Then, it's on to Steamed Venus Clams & Mussels. Ladled atop the shells are sublime chunks of Portuguese sausage, which somehow meld perfectly with the clams and mussels. And, the fennel saffron broth they serve with these fortunate shells is something I would drink with a straw ... all day long. Chef Rainer simply shrugs, "It's just fennel, white wine, saffron and butter, really ... and at the end, lots of fresh lemon juice."

A Solid Variety of Entrées

In the entrées category, the chefs agree that the Grilled Cheese and Beach Burger are well-deserving favorites among diners.

I choose the Vancouver Island King Salmon, instead. The fresh salmon arrives atop a generous swirl of English pea coulis, tender Oyster mushrooms and roasted, slightly caramelized Cipollini onions. Beautiful.

It's not difficult to sit here, lulled by sunshine, the ocean lapping at the shore, enjoying what has arguably become one of the better food experiences in Laguna Beach. Thanks to Chef Rainer and a team that never stopped believing, it's great to see The Deck smoothly firing on all cylinders.

At Press Time: White House Restaurant Serves Up More Than Great Drinks

350 S. Coast Highway, Laguna Beach, CA 92651
(949) 494-8088

Just as we were going to press, I managed a dining review on the extensive lunch and dinner menu at The White House Restaurant. Family owned for decades, these people know how to dish up hearty, flavorful food. See LagunaBeachBest.com and search "White House."

Juice & Shakes
154 S. Coast Highway • Laguna Beach

Best *Coffee* Houses & *Breakfasts*

Juice & Shakes
154 S. Coast Highway • Laguna Beach

ANDREE'S PATISSERIE

1456 S. Coast Highway, Laguna Beach, CA 92651
(949) 494-1577

Pastry average: \$2 – \$4
Hours: Mondays, 7:35 a.m. – noon Tuesday – Friday, 7:35 a.m. – 3:00 p.m. Saturday, 7:35 a.m. – 1:00 p.m. Closed Sunday
Noise level at busiest: 2 out of 10
Good for kids? Yes
Dogs: No

As his regulars cross the Andree's Patisserie threshold, he is already bagging their favorite item. He greets each customer with a happy grin, and gestures with the bakery bag in hand, filled with flaky goodness. This person always wants a Bear Claw. That one prefers the plain croissant. This one is in for his turkey sandwich (no cheese).

For Ron Reno, sole proprietor of Andree's Patisserie, this is what running a small town bakery is all about. "I have an appreciation for the people who choose me," he says. "It's important that every person who walks in my door knows that."

For 32 years ...1,636 weeks ... and nearly 10,000 days, Ron Reno has been mixing, baking and serving his famed pastries and coffee in this Laguna Beach historic location. He is, quite literally, chief, cook and bottle washer. On the rare occasions that he's chosen to take a week-long vacation or been forced into a 4-week leave for ACL surgery, he simply closes his blue door and attaches a note to its front with the date of his return.

Ron Reno is, otherwise, the one and only person you will see at Andree's Patisserie, from 7:35 a.m. to about 2 p.m., every day of the week but Sunday. On Sunday, Ron rests.

In 1981, Ron took over this famed bakery, initially in place since the late 1940s as an adjunct bakery for the restaurant next door (the restaurant was named Andree's, which is now Selanne's Steak Tavern).

Every pre-dawn morning, Monday through Saturday, Ron bakes "271 items" for weekdays, and doubles the amount for Saturdays. A variety of muffins. Three kinds of croissants. Three kinds of cookies (Almond Biscotti counts as one). A crowd of Danishes. The inimitable Bear Claw. Elephant Ears. Three kinds of sandwiches, their ingredients piled high inside freshly baked slices of Ron's secret recipe potato bread. The baked riches neatly stack themselves, shelf upon shelf, readied for another day of happy buyers.

At the holidays, Ron's faithful followers spread the love by buying up hundreds of his fabled holiday cookies and pies to share with family, coworkers and friends.

Freshly baked cutout cookies with thick frosting shoulder their way into the store's pastry bins at all the major holidays, even the Fourth of July. He creates cookie stacks in cellophane wrap, and they disappear as quickly as they're bagged and gift-tied.

At Thanksgiving and Christmas, Ron shifts into high-production mode, baking 100-140 apple, pecan and pumpkin pies within two days of the given holiday. While this is in addition to his usual daily baking, he says it never feels like overload. "When it's pie-making time, it signifies that time of year again, and it's a special time to me," he notes. "It's like welcoming old friends back into my bakery."

Where many Laguna Beach bakeries have been vanquished by larger commercial organizations, and where bakeries everywhere have come to rely on third-party sourcing to fill their daily pastry bins, Ron Reno will continue to wake at 4:00 a.m. and roll his doughs by hand until he's simply not able to perform the work any longer.

"I can't imagine retiring," he says. "When I had ACL surgery, I spent four long weeks sitting on my couch, watching each day go by. I'd watch the light change by degrees as it made its way across my backyard until it was dark. I'd go to bed, and I'd get up again to go sit on the couch. It was my own personal *Groundhog Day* movie."

"This place ..." he gestures to his pastry bins, the window counter with its sentry stools, "This place here in Laguna Beach is the movie I want to see every day of my life."

Photo credit: Mary Hurlbut, MaryHurlbutphoto.com

CAFÉ ANASTASIA

460 Ocean Ave., Laguna Beach, CA 92651
(949) 497-8903

Breakfast average: $10 – $13
Hours: 7 a.m. – 3 p.m.
Noise level at busiest: 2 out of 10 on patio, 4 out of 10 inside
Good for kids? It's OK but kids can get fidgety
Dogs: Yes
Menu: www.LagunaBeachBest.com/Menus/Café-Anastasia

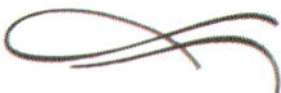

This last weekend, my BFF, Lisa, and I decided on a spontaneous weekend breakfast out in Laguna Beach. Now, because this is rare and special treat, we had to choose a breakfast restaurant here in town that does more than dole out a couple eggs and strips of bacon. Anastasia's on Ocean in downtown Laguna Beach was – of course – the answer.

Anastasia Cafe sits at the end of Ocean Avenue, about 3 blocks from Main Beach in the downtown village of Laguna Beach. Because it's somewhat tucked in, it tends to cater more to residents than out-of-towners simply because we know where to find it. It's a gracious, sophisticated favorite that offers one of the most unique breakfast menus in Laguna Beach.

Anastasia is a combo upscale clothing boutique and restaurant. When owners Zore and Amir Gharavi first came to Laguna in the early 1980s, they started with a clothing boutique, importing some of the finest names in designer clothing (Vivienne Westwood, Unholy Matrimony, Rick Owens, Issey Miyake, Gareth Pugh and Peachoo + Krejberg, to name a few). In a matter of months, they had developed a loyal following from Los Angeles, San Francisco, and all parts of the world.

The Gharavis moved to their Ocean Avenue location in the late 1990s and, in 1997, opened their restaurant adjacent to the expanded clothing boutique. The Anastasia Cafe has a Euro flair to it … something you'd find in upscale regions of the south of France or Milan, perhaps. The couple developed a menu around Mediterranean and French breakfast and lunch foods, and the place has been packed since its first day's opening.

Insider note: Lately, the team has introduced 3 Off-Menu Specials that are racking up serous popularity points.

Machaca – scrambled eggs with super lean, shredded beef, diced onions, peppers and chilies.

Eggs Benedict – two poached eggs bathed in a rich benedict sauce, but perched this time on a bed of Italian sausage and crisp hash browns.

Chorizo & Eggs – my personal favorite, this dish offers a spectacular blend of eggs scrambled with Anastasia's own family chorizo recipe – it's super light, lean, non-greasy and happily missing some of those animal parts you'd rather not know were in regular Chorizo. Then, they fold in onions, red bell peppers, cilantro, chunks of potatoes, and top it with feta cheese, avocado and a dollop of sour cream.

Sheer heaven. I've had this dish twice and have managed to tackle about one-third of the heaping serving before giving up and boxing the rest. It serves up quite beautifully as a leftover, I assure you.

Kiko, Anastasia's unflappable greeter, order taker, cashier and drinks king has worked at Anastasia's nearly as long as the chairs and tables have. He says all three Off-Menu breakfast "trials" are selling off the charts and, though neck-and-neck in sales, the Chorizo dish has a slight lead. Let's hope Anastasia's makes all three of these gourmet breakfast additions a permanent part of their menu.

Anastasia isn't a "turn-em-and-burn-em" kind of breakfast joint. Don't expect your egg dish to arrive, slightly slopped, in less than 3 minutes. You may wait 15 minutes for your plates to arrive, and when they DO arrive, they're a work of art. So, while you're waiting, sit back and people watch, or pop over to the connected boutique for some new seasonal fashions.

Best Poached Egg Dishes in Laguna Beach

Anastasia offers phenomenal omelets and egg dishes, with FIVE different poached egg dishes (their Eggs Anna is my favorite with poached eggs on a tower of arugula and lean prosciutto). But ... you really can't miss the construction zone plate of Caramel French Toast (with warm caramel drizzle sauce on the side, simply killer.)

Further, expect to pay an average $12-$17 per plate. Anastasia makes no excuses and it doesn't have to. This Laguna Beach gem is truly a *piece de resistance* in our lovely town.

Anastasia Cafe in Laguna Beach is open through lunch, with a popular line up of sandwiches, salads and pastas. As expected, the Anastasia afternoon fare is as original and meticulously presented as its breakfast counterpart. Anastasia's is also dog friendly. Your pooch is more than welcome to join you in the outside patio seating area.

COYOTE GRILL

31621 S. Coast Highway, Laguna Beach, CA 92651
(949) 499-4033

Breakfast, average $8 – $14
Hours: Breakfast 7 a.m. – noon, and Sat/Sun 7 a.m. – 2 p.m.
Lunch and dinner also served, see page 62
Noise level at busiest: In the bar: 9 out of 10,
In the restaurant: 6 out of 10
Good for kids? Yep
Dogs: No

Menu: www.LagunaBeachBest.com/Menus/Coyote-Grill

I happen to love that the Coyote Grill is so close to my home because it's the only restaurant serving up breakfast in all of South Laguna Beach. It's a great, hearty breakfast, too! (For my review on lunch and dinner offerings at Coyote Grill, see *Casual Dining*.)

Coyote Grill is a small, friendly place with a front, rather crowded neighborhood bar, and plenty of restaurant seating toward the back. The Grill also has a great enclosed patio with an awesome

ocean view. It handles another 12 tables of so, and in the winter, the huge fireplace at the south end delivers some serious heat.

Breakfast starts up at 7 a.m., and though it's fairly easy to find seating on weekdays, the weekends see lines of hungry diners snaking from the place at about 9:30 a.m. Coyote pays tribute to its Mexican roots with large portions of great Chicken or Beef Machaca, Chilaquilas, homemade Chorizo & Eggs, and Huevos Rancheros.

For those more reticent about spice and peppers in a breakfast dish, Coyote is happy to serve up more "Americanized" breakfasts, too.

For starters, the Banana Pancakes are a memorable boatload of flapjack goodness. The Coyote Special Waffle, the Philly Eggs or any of the enormous omelettes are hearty and filling. Everything comes with options for potatoes, beans and tortillas or toast, so don't think you're eating lightly here.

Coyote also mixes up a memorable Bloody Mary, and offers a Kona Coffee treat from its own coffee patch in (of all places), Kona. The servers have been here for years and service is usually very prompt, even at the busiest times. I wouldn't say that the Coyote Grill makes an art form out of breakfast like some of our Laguna Beach restaurants, but it certainly provides solid, down-home cookin', Mexican style.

GG'S BISTRO

540 S. Coast Highway, Laguna Beach, CA 92651
(949) 494-9306
Breakfast: Only on Sundays,
average $6 – $14
Noise level at busiest: On the patio: 2 out of 10,
In the restaurant: 2 out of 10
Good for kids? Yep
Dogs: Dogs can sit outside on the other side of the patio open fence

Menu: www.LagunaBeachBest.com/Menus/GGs-Bistro

For nearly a decade, the two husband-and-wife teams of GG's Italian Mediterranean Bistro have managed to keep the life in the main level of this 540 South Coast Highway complex.

GG's Bistro splits its restaurant between an in-house dining and bar establishment tucked in the corner, and an upfront patio dining experience. While GG's has become a locals' favorite for lunch, happy hour (M-F) and dinner, I particularly love GG's for Sunday morning breakfast.

Some days, I'll just pop in for their Turkish coffee or tea, and enjoy their fresh baked baguettes with homemade strawberry jam. For me, it feels that I've nestled myself into a streetside café in Europe, and that ambience alone is enough to make my day. But, in most cases, I can't pass on the many great dishes GG's Bistro serves up.

It All Started in a Turkish Fencing Factory ...

GG's Bistro came about when two brothers, Bulent and Ragip Gundogar, decided it was time to get out of their successful fencing factory business in Turkey and do something else. In fact, not only were they ready to *do* something else, they were ready to *move* somewhere else, too.

Convinced that their good partnership in the commercial industry could parlay to commercial cooking, the two couples (Hande with Bulent and Franziska with Ragip) decided they'd open a restaurant in Southern California together, and in September, 2004, they up and moved! By February 2005, the brothers in fencing had become brothers in sauces and skillets.

"As soon as we signed the lease, we hired a Turkish Culinary Art teacher," says Ragip. "He helped us for a month establishing our menu and training us on the line. Obviously, it was invaluable to us!"

"Euro Food Americanized"

As I've noted, the GG's Bistro breakfast menu is served just on Sundays from 9 a.m. to 11:30 a.m. The ingredients are super fresh, the eggs are whipped light beyond belief and the hash browns are officially the Eighth Deadly Sin. They are buttery, rich and crisped just perfectly.

The Turkish Pan Fried Eggs arrive still in their pan, nuzzled next to perfectly grilled Turkish sausage and a heap of hash browns. It's easily my favorite on the menu.

The GG's Omelets are healthy affairs, too, and subdivided by country (French, Italian, American, Mediterranean, etc.). The Mediterranean Plate is another crowd favorite, heaped with Feta cheese chunks, Kalamata olives, cucumber slices and Mediterranean style Roma tomatoes.

I haven't tried their popular pancakes yet, but I've dug into GG's French Toast and am happy to report that it's just like my Mom used to make (only GG's is friendlier with the powdered sugar, Mom).

The servers are unhurried and they have no intention of bustling you along. The music overhead is a mix of light classical and Parisian. The diners tend to be European themselves, and they sip and sun and talk world news in their lovely accents. Were it not for the lazy Sunday traffic passing by on PCH below, you might think you've actually found your way to Turkey instead of the other way around.

JUICE & SHAKES

154 S. Coast Highway, Laguna Beach, CA 92651
(949) 400-2222

Breakfast, average $3 – $8
Hours: Sunday – Thursday, 7:00 a.m. – 7:00 p.m., Fridays & Saturdays, 7:00 a.m. – 9:00 p.m
Noise level at busiest: In the bar: 9 out of 10,
In the restaurant: 1 out of 10
Good for kids? Yep
Dogs: No

Menu: www.LagunaBeachBest.com/Menus/Juice-and-Shakes

If you know anything about the brilliant Chris Keller, you know one thing: The guy isn't just going to slap up a random eatery, even if it's just a small juice bar.

Since Chris first arrived in Laguna Beach with plans for the Rooftop Bar and the revamp of K'ya in the lobby of Casa Resorts, he's never done anything randomly or half-cocked. As he's opened more restaurants, taken on more hotels, revamped the renowned Marine Room and participated in just about every board the city has to offer, Chris is as methodical and deliberate as he is fast-moving and decisive.

Even after Chris took on the old Haagen Dazs property next to the Laguna movie theater in 2013, he and his wife, Amy, were in no hurry to slap something together.

Today's Hottest Health Trend in an Old-Fashioned Setting

Finally, in late 2014, Juice & Shakes opened its doors. And, even though

Laguna Beach totes at least six other juice bars, Juice & Shakes is (not surprisingly) a one-of-a-kind, standout personality, offering fully organic cold-pressed juices, shakes, ice cream acai and pitaya bowls and kombucha shots.

For starters, the place is a spotless, nostalgic rendition of a small town, old-fashioned soda fountain shop. From white marble tops to gleaming chrome fixtures and whimsical draft spigots for the flavored kombucha and organic coffee, it's as charming and welcoming as the staff behind the counter.

As Chris and Amy "researched" their way through every sort of juice concoction, they turned their home kitchen into a research station all its own, too.

"We wanted to set ourselves apart with some fun combinations," says Amy. "Take the #8, for instance, a super-smooth and yummy combo of yellow pepper, apple, lime ands turmeric. I claim it's my favorite ... until I try the coconut-apple-ginger juice. I claim *that's* my favorite until I try the #6 with carrot, orange, apple, turmeric and cinnamon. I claim *that's* my new favorite until I try the #4 with pineapple, carrot, beet, lemon, romaine and ginger.

Finally, I give up claiming my favorite.

Once you see the cold-press juicer crowded in the back of the Juice & Shakes store, you know Chris Keller has expansion up his sleeve. The machine is one of the largest cold pressers in the industry, able to squeeze whole pineapples and bushels of beets in mere seconds.

"We plan to have at least one other Juice & Shakes store in another location in 2015," says Amy. The couple says they will also be introducing raw food salads and "grab and go" entrees, too.

While Amy's quinoa salads and Root Soup temporarily wait on a back burner, she and Chris have steamed ahead with acai, pitaya and super food bowls (the latter called The Superbowl).

They dish up a Superbowl with acai, greens, blueberry, banana and coconut water topped with banana, blueberry, almonds, walnuts, coconut, agave, chia and flax seeds. (Whew.)

The Pitaya (dragonfruit) Bowl is gorgeous neon pink dragonfruit blended with banana, mango and coconut water. It's topped with banana, granola, coconut flakes, agave and chia seeds. Both options are super fresh and crazy delicious.

For me, though, the crowning delight is the flavored Kombucha on draft, with taste options of strawberry, "trilogy" and gingerade. Leave it to Chris Keller to dream up draft pours of this renowned "elixir of life."

Chris and Amy offer free samples of any juice drink, and are selling "Juice Flights," which allow a formal tasting of up to eight juices. "We know we have something for everyone here, even the people who have never really tried juices or juicing as a regular part of their diet," says Amy.

"We just want to be able to show people how quickly their bodies can change and heal, and everything here at Juice & Shakes can help make that happen."

LAGUNA COFFEE COMPANY

1050 S. Coast Highway, Laguna Beach, CA 92651
(949) 494-6901

Average: $2 – $8
Hours: Mon – Wed, 6 a.m. – 6 p.m.; Thurs & Fri, 6 a.m. – 8 p.m.;
Sat 6:30 a.m. – 8 p.m., Sun, 7 a.m. – 6 p.m.
Noise level at busiest: 1 out of 10 on patio, 5 out of 10 inside
Good for kids? Yes
Dogs: Yes
Wi-Fi: Yes

Menu: www.LagunaBeachBest.com/Menus/Laguna-Coffee

One of the finest "indys" in coffeehouses in Laguna, I always recommend Laguna Coffee, a small shop tucked between Oak and Brook streets on the north side of PCH. Owned by Paul & Cathy Ackley,

the staff couldn't be nicer, and Paul roasts the coffee beans there in the front room (find THAT somewhere else!). Small wonder, then, that you see stacks of people lined up in the mornings for their favorite cup of joe.

Once you have tasted their smooth blends, you'll be buying pounds of coffee to tuck in your suitcase for the kitchen back home ... and a few friends' kitchens, too. In addition to its famous coffee lineup, Laguna Coffee also offers a vast variety of teas, in-house daily baked pastries, and light breakfast dishes (yogurt sundaes, bagel scrambles, etc.)

Laguna Coffee has such an interesting blend of local, friendly folks – some uber-wealthy that you'd never guess owned more than a coffee cup themselves; some artistic types; some all-business commuters (the few hardy souls that actually leave town to go work somewhere else); and a healthy draught of eclectics all around.

Of course, tourists and visitors wander in, too, and once they understand that this is no Starbucks (thank heavens), they're easily taken in by the friendly staffers headed up by René and Peggy, Sylvan's famous pastries and cookies, and Kevin Montoya's deadly cakes and raspberry muffins (see *Snacks & Desserts*). Add to that the chatty, rambling ambience of people and dogs, and you just can't find a better heartbeat anywhere in Laguna Beach.

Insider Tips: On Saturday, Laguna Coffee rocks with a mornings collection of professional jazz musicians who just decided to hang out and play. (See *Events* for details.)

LAGUNA FEASTS

801 Glenneyre Street, Laguna Beach, CA 92651
(949) 494-0642 for take out

Breakfast average: $4 – $7
Hours: Breakfast 7 a.m. – 11 a.m., Lunch/Dinner also served
Noise level at busiest: 2 out of 10
Good for kids? Yep
Dogs: Yes on patio Menu:

www.LagunaBeachBest.com/Menus/Laguna-Feasts

Let's just say two things about Laguna Feasts right from the start:

#1. People may say they serve "authentic Mexican food." Trust me. Nothing more authentic than here at this tiny little place, Laguna Feasts.

#2. While friends tout every dish on the Feasts menu as delicious and seriously underpriced for serving portions, I haven't been able to visit the Feasts boys for anything other than breakfast. I can assure you, though, that there is no better breakfast burrito in town than here.

Now, to get on with the formal review:
As if last weekend wasn't beautiful enough, I discovered that my favorite

breakfast joint for the most amazing breakfast burritos in Laguna Beach is now open on SUNDAYS, too. Once you have a breakfast burrito at Feasts, you'll know why I'm doing the Snoopy Dance over here.

Here's the straight fact: After a long night at the Sandpiper or White House, you might be one of those folks who feels a need for a good, hearty breakfast the morning after.

Now, granted, most of Laguna Beach's breakfast nooks are just as extreme in their creative menu efforts as their fine dining counterparts, but Laguna Feasts is one small little corner joint that serves up the meanest, sauciest, steamiest breakfast burrito without a single nod to poached anything. They're not about the fluff – they're all about the food. In fact, Laguna Feasts Mexican Food is so South-of-the-border authentic that if its counter staff WERE to offer an apology, it would come at you in Spanish.

Walk into Feasts at the corner of Glenneyre and St. Ann's and you're walking into Old World Mexico – and these folks aren't even trying. Small Formica tables and chairs crowd the interior and side patio, while Spanish TV soap operas blare from the TV hung in the corner. The place is as neat as a pin, though, and you'll be greeted with a wide, cordial smile.

Choose your breakfast burrito stuffed with egg and your choice of meat – ham, sausage, chorizo, or chicken or beef machaca – and ask for a green chili smother. (If you're really going to go all out … and like it matters anyway with all the calories you're already committed to consuming … get the sausage with an extra bacon striddle.) Then, let the griddle master work his masterpiece as you take in the Spanish soap opera of the hour. Three minutes later, you'll have a 2-pound beauty in your hands, steaming with fresh chili and about a half pound of cheese.

Say no more. Nothing like it in Laguna Beach.

MADISON'S SQUARE & GARDEN CAFE

320 N. Coast Highway, Laguna Beach, CA 92651
(949) 494-0137

Breakfast/lunch menu average: $6 – $14
Hours: 8 a.m. – 2:30 p.m., Closed Tuesdays
Noise level at busiest: 2 out of 10
Good for kids? Yes
Dogs: Oh, yes

Menu: www.LagunaBeachBest.com/Menus/Madisons-Square-Café

If I lived closer to North Laguna Beach, I think I'd while half of my every day away at Jon Madison's eclectic décor shop and cafe.

The place looks like a garden and yard décor shop from the sidewalk on PCH, but step inside and you have this crazy, incredible selection of home décor items AND a tiny kitchen of helpful staffers waiting to take your breakfast or lunch order.

This is a small, but oh so powerful menu. For breakfast, I would tell you to go no further than the extraordinary Ricotta Pancakes flavored with lemon, ginger and topped with fresh berries, whipped butter and maple syrup ... ok, maybe I WILL tell you to go no further than this ... BUT you must ALSO, at some time, try the fluffy German Apple Pancake and the Cinnamon Swirl French Toast, too.

If you're not into immeasurably sound calories for breakfast, try Jon's own Eggs Benedict, his Vegetable Frittata or the Madison Huevos Rancheros. Madison's offers a substantial lunch menu of creative salads, burgers, chicken sandwiches and grilled fresh fish dishes, but I have to tell you honestly ... I rarely get farther than the Ricotta Pancakes.

While you're waiting for your food, take 3 or 10 circles of the grounds in hopes that the 8th or 9th trip around will ensure that you've managed to see everything in this fun and whimsical home and garden décor store.

There is no inside café seating at Madison's. You have to settle, poor you, for sitting at any number of patio tables, surrounded by simply extraordinary Buddhas, ready-made waterfalls, monstrous wind chimes, and hundreds of fun garden accoutrements.

Note: Jon Madison is a huge fan of dogs but from a regular attendee's perspective, be sure your dog plays well with others as this is more of a happy, bounding dog park than a couple dogs resigned to their short leashes wrapped around their owners' chairs.

MOSAIC BAR & GRILLE, THE MONTAGE RESORT

30801 Coast Highway, Laguna Beach, CA 92651
(949) 715-6020

Breakfast is only served on Sundays,
though a lunch menu is served every day
Hours: 9:30 a.m. – 11:00 a.m.
Noise level at busiest: 1 out of 10
Good for kids? Yes
Dogs: No

Yet another stellar find at the Montage Resort, Chef Miguel Ruiz is making his mark on the poolside Mosaic Bar & Grille.

Now, normally the Mosaic is a great kickback location for casual lunch fare and sunset drinks at its cabana. On Sunday mornings, though, Chef Ruiz turns up the love with a Breakfast Sandwich that leaves me ... well, almost wordless.

We've all had a million breakfast sandwiches in our day. They're a staple at every fast food restaurant known to mankind, and we've probably all cooked an attempt of our own in the comfort of our own kitchens. What

Chef Ruiz has created here simply defies any breakfast sandwich I've yet come to know.

If you've read my other reviews about the Montage in this book, you've probably come to the rightful conclusion that the Montage can't do anything on a small scale. It's a massive, opulent resort and, apparently, the chefs are driven to produce food fare of similar weight and heft.

The Mosaic Breakfast Sandwich has to weigh at least a pound. It is awesome to simply look upon. Once you fork your way into it (I have no idea how anyone could just eat this like a regular breakfast sandwich), it is even more magnificence. I guess in plain terms it's something of a BLT, but the bacon is this slow-cured, thick crunchy stuff with neighborly fresh avocado, a perfectly cooked egg and some sort of secret crazy sauce that could be sold on the black market for a lot of money. It arrives nestled in a freshly baked bun that offers just the right amount of bread, and not one flavor overwhelms the other.

I don't know how he does it. I've tried to imitate it, believe me and, repeatedly, I sigh in surrender and make a beeline for the Mosaic.

Life in Laguna Beach

Michael Alten,
Plein Air artist

ORANGE INN

703 S. Coast Highway, Laguna Beach, CA 92651
(949) 494-6085

Breakfast/lunch menu average: $3 – $15
Hours: 6 a.m. – 5 p.m.
Noise level at busiest: 3 out of 10
Good for kids? Yes
Dogs: Yes

Menu: www.LagunaBeachBest.com/Menus/Orange-Inn-Laguna-Beach

OK, let's correct the first big fallacy. Laguna Beach's Orange Inn is not an inn. It's a longtime locals' favorite for breakfast, fresh juices and yummy sandwiches.

Aside from its fantastic coffee – organic with a hint of hickory, and definitely in my Top 5 Coffees in Laguna Beach – the Orange Inn welcomes a long line of locals and tourists who share an addiction for the shop's early-morning baked oversized fruit muffins (try the Peach Muffin), monstrous cinnamon rolls, homemade granola and a variety of egg dishes.

This place was first established in 1931 as a refreshment stop between Newport Beach and

The Guinness World Record Holder for the Orange Smoothie!

When the Orange Inn moved to its current location, John and Kathy Bodrero took over as the owners. Kathy came up with her super-secret granola recipe and decided other unique menu items while John is officially in the Guinness record books as the "Original Founder of the Smoothie" ... And what an Orange Inn Smoothie it is – Strawberries, bananas, dates, fresh orange juice and bee pollen all whipped up without a stitch of sugar or artificial anything. Small wonder every juice, ice cream and yogurt place in the world decided to steal the idea from our Laguna Beach Bodrero genius. It doesn't matter what they do – this smoothie is not only historical, it's a sublime experience.

Laguna Beach for cowboys and field hands. Over the years, it gained immense popularity as a roadside attraction to workers, celebrities and tourists alike. In 1986, it moved to the heart of Laguna Beach on the ocean side of PCH at Cleo Street – it sits right across from the Ralph's grocery store.

While tourists largely dominate the Orange Inn in the summer and during weekends, we Laguna Beach locals love congregating here on our early morning weekdays. John, the owner, loves greeting his regulars, many of whom have been coming here for 20 years or more. In turn, the regulars have all gotten to know each other and it's a constant activity of handshakes, bear hugs and kisses. The Orange Inn is like walking into your neighborhood surf shack on the morning of a classic, incoming swell. It's just got the vibe, man.

THE RANCH

31106 S. Coast Highway, Laguna Beach, CA 92651
(949) 499-2271

Breakfast/lunch menu average: $10 – $18
Hours: vary by season, call for specifics
Noise level at busiest: 1 out of 10
Good for kids? Yes
Dogs: No (too close to the golf course)

Menu: www.LagunaBeachBest.com/Menus/The-Ranch-Laguna-Beach

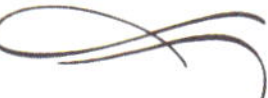

From the beginning, The Ranch's focus and vision has been on "retrofying" its historical property while still putting nifty and thoughtful innovations and surprise in play. Take, for instance, The Ranch's newly renovated Ben's Pantry in the old coffee shop's location, and the daily breakfast menu they launched … everything they do here at The Ranch is a lovely mix of nostalgia and creative, modernized craftery.

For The Ranch's Director of Culinary Operations, 36-year-old Camron Woods, it offers a perfect opportunity to meld "tradition and creative freedom" in the menus, too. "We have the freedom here to do some great craft cooking, to create dishes that are truly a step away from the norm. Sometimes, we let the tradition stand alone, and other times, we bring a little innovation to the tradition."

And this, my friends, is where the fun begins in the breakfast menu at The Ranch. Case in point: The "healthier version" of Smoked Salmon Benedict. Chef Camron house-cures the salmon over a 3-day timeframe in a mix of brown sugar, salt, lemons, limes and oranges.

To create his hollandaise sauce, he ages an original champagne vinegar base and tosses dill into the mix. And, he won't butter the English muffin underneath ("Poached eggs come with a lot of water moisture and, unless you dry-toast the muffin, you're going to get sog somewhere in the middle," he explains).

End result: One of the best Eggs Benedict I've experienced in years.

The Chicken & Waffles are a loving forkful of Southern love. Piping hot Belgian waffles are topped with tender chunks of fresh-out-of-the-fryer fried chicken, which is then generously swathed in biscuits-and-gravy kind of homemade gravy. Chef is merciful at least, in offering a mound of whipped butter and fresh maple syrup as side dishes.

Chef's side dish of grits makes no excuses for itself, either. It arrives in a small skillet, steaming and blanketed in a sheen of cheese. So often a misunderstood and misrepresented dish, these grits are mighty and proud. Wow, are they good.

Then, yet another piece de résistance – Pastry Chef Mary Catherine's Smoked Bourbon Bacon Cinnamon Roll.

As it turns out, Chef Mary is actually Camron's wife – the two met in Atlanta while working at The Four Seasons, moved to San Diego in 2007 to open the Grand Del Mar resort, married in 2010, and then moved up to the Laguna Beach area at the start of this year.

I, for one, am terribly glad she followed him if just for the resulting Cinnamon Roll. It's a crazy-good combined chefs' effort of her pastry skills and Camron's love for "real bacon."

For his side of the bargain, he cures the pork in a salt and sugar mix for two days. Then, he rubs the bacon down in bourbon, lets that air dry until a pellicle skin forms, and eventually pops it in the smoker. The end result adorns the giant roll like the crown on a triumphant king's head.

"There's something about Camron's cooking that just has gusto to it," says Kurt Bjorkman, The Ranch General Manager. "To be a great restaurant in a hotel resort environment, you have to have a unique quality about yourself," says Bjorkman. "But we all wanted this restaurant to be able to stand on its own, too, and that … I think … requires an even greater amount of passion from your Chef."

Mission accomplished, Chef. What a great new breakfast and lunch venue for locals and visitors alike.

ROOFTOP

1289 S. Coast Highway (top of La Casa del Camino
Laguna Beach, CA 92651
Reservations only taken for parties of 6 or more: (949) 497-2446

Breakfast, lunch, average $9 – $15
Hours: Breakfast Saturday and Sunday ONLY, 9 a.m. – 11:30 a.m.,
Lunch 11:30 a.m. – 2:30 p.m.
Noise level at busiest: 2 out of 10 (for breakfast and lunch, not the Happy Hour)
Good for kids? Yes
Dogs: Yes
Wi-Fi: Yes

Menu: www.LagunaBeachBest.com/Menus/Rooftop-Laguna-Beach

Nothing could be finer than starting your weekend morning with unobstructed views of the Pacific and an oh-so-fine breakfast laid before you. In my opinion, Rooftop Restaurant, at the top of La Casa del Camino Hotel, provides the very best breakfast view in all of Laguna Beach, and its breakfast menu is very decent as well.

I don't know how far you have read into these many entries of mine, but sooner or later you're going to discover that I'm a fan of Chef Craig

Connole, the creative genius behind two restaurants here in town. So, while I'm quite apologetic for what I'm about to say, we're just going to have to face facts from the start here:

It doesn't matter if you have been making scrambled egg dishes in your kitchen for the last 20 years ... Chef Craig Connole is likely to have you beat. It's why I leave my own panoramic view in my own Laguna Beach home to head to Craig's Rooftop restaurant.

Along with six Scrambles to choose from, the Rooftop menu offers a variety of "standard breakfast fare" – i.e., Huevos Rancheros, Breakfast Burrito, French Toast – none of which emerges from the kitchen looking or tasting standard at all. I gave up trying to explain this about Chef Craig a long time ago. The man loves creating and plating at an entirely different level, and we're the winners for it.

Life in Laguna Beach

In downtown Laguna Beach, enjoy strolling the Dawson Cole Sculpture Garden

SAPPHIRE

1200 S. Coast Highway, #101, Laguna Beach, CA 92651
(949) 715-9888

Menu average: $12 – $18
Hours: Weekend brunch, 10:00 a.m. – 3:00 p.m.
Noise level at busiest: 3 out of 10
Good for kids? Yes
Dogs: Yes

Menu: www.LagunaBeachBest.com/Menus/Sapphire

At Sapphire last weekend, I asked a manager and a hostess what they would recommend above all else on their brunch menu. They both said "oatmeal."

Oatmeal. Really?

As it turns out, Chef Azmin Ghahreman doesn't seem to know much about the kind of oatmeal most of us were raised on. He and his Chef de Cuisine got to talking about how they were raised on "savory" oatmeal and ended up producing an oatmeal mixed with crispy pork belly, kale, Pecorino cheese, garlic chips and a soft poached egg (to boot).

Now that's an oatmeal! And this is Sapphire Laguna, whose simplest concoctions of eggs, breakfast meats and pancakes offers your taste buds a wealth of celebration and happy awe.

Since its opening in 2007, Sapphire hasn't missed a beat. From the start, Chef Azmin imbedded a fresh and innovative international flair to his menus, having served in top-level culinary positions all around the world.

Understandably, most raves and accolades rain down about the highly-acclaimed, ever-changing dinner menu. The Sapphire brunch menu, though, is the bridge that crosses the moat, leaving ordinary fare behind and heralding that hint of sumptuous fare to come.

True to its international promise, breakfast items vary enormously. The Oatmeal could quite possibly be the most unique breakfast item I've yet tried in Laguna Beach. The Fried Chicken N' Cheddar Biscuit, though, has no intention of taking second fiddle. It is a pile of scrambled eggs and green onion-sausage gravy ladled atop freshly baked cheddar biscuits. This, in itself, would be a most satisfying exercise, but the crispy/moist fried chicken takes you to the mat.

On the lunch side of the brunch, you just can't pass on the Sapphire Kobe Havarti Cheeseburger – it's actually ranked in my "Top 4 Gourmet Burgers of Laguna Beach" (see www.LagunaBeachBest.com).

The Sapphire Kobe burger is a melt-in-your-mouth kind of experience. Its mild manner is complemented with caramelized onion and peppery arugula and … uhmm … garlic fries (which I promise we did not wolf down).

In the end, Sapphire is more than just a great treat on a Saturday or Sunday – it's that moat crossing to how a dining experience really should be.

15FIFTYFIVE: LAGUNA BEACH LOUNGE, SURF & SAND RESORT

1555 S. Coast Highway, Laguna Beach, CA 92651
(949) 376-2779

Coffee average: $2 – $5
Hours: Daily, 6:30 a.m. – 6:00 p.m.
Noise level at busiest: 1 out of 10
Good for kids? Yes
Dogs: Yes
Wi-Fi: Yes

I love my favorite coffeehouses here in town, but once you get to know the locals, there isn't a lot of opportunity to stuff yourself in a corner and play anonymous because every third person is saying "howdy." Granted, this is a great thing, but once in a while you just want a place to sip your coffee and think.

My dear friend, Diane Alms, reminded me of a perfectly "zen" place for coffee, and it's the direction we scuttle when we're due for a chatty catch-up. It's a place I doubt many locals wander to (but we should) – the outdoor 15FiftyFive Lounge at the Surf & Sand Resort.

The first true resort here in town, The Surf & Sand is opulence at its finest, and it's quite warm and welcoming to locals and passerby. The resort's 15FiftyFive Lounge, just to the right of the resort's main entry, is normally a hopping place with live music at sunset. In the mornings, though, it is a lovely, quiet bask on cushy couches with a close-up view of our glorious ocean.

Tucked just across from the outdoor lounge is a tiny coffee shop, Pacific Perks, with an equally perky barista who whips up any coffee, espresso, latte, shaken-not-stirred order you can devise. Then, just stroll out and choose your couch, whether by the outdoor fireplace or overlooking the ocean. Very few people congregate here in the early morning hours, even during high tourist season, so you have plenty of time to talk, think and plan.

Life in Laguna Beach

The tiny Brown's Park, almost directly across from Gelato Paradiso. It's worth a visit.

THE WHITE HOUSE

340 S. Coast Highway, Laguna Beach, CA 92651
(949) 494-8088

Breakfast average, $8-$10, Weekend Brunch, $8 – $13
Hours: Breakfast weekdays, 8 – 11 a.m.,
Weekend brunch, 8:00 a.m. – 4:00 p.m.
Noise level at busiest: 5 out of 10 on patio because of PCH traffic,
3 out of 10 inside
Good for kids? Yes
Dogs: No (most folks leash their dogs to nearby parking meters, which are just a few feet away from the patio seating)

Menu: www.LagunaBeachBest.com/Menus/White-House-Laguna-Beach

The White House Restaurant has called Laguna Beach home since 1918, and it fires on all cylinders – breakfast, lunch, happy hour, dinner and late-night live music. This review, though, is strictly about its breakfast and brunch menu. I honestly don't think many locals think of the White House for breakfast, which I'm convinced is one of its better inventions.

I like the White House because it offers a much larger breakfast and brunch menu than most of its breakfast peers in Laguna Beach. It's also very reasonably priced for a serious heaping of very good food. Although I believe the White House is much more innovative, fresh and tastier than chains like Ruby's or Denny's, it offers that great menu variety that is apt to please any palette in your group.

If you're craving Eggs Benedict, there's really no better option in Laguna Beach – the White House serves up at least five perfectly crafted versions

of the English muffin-poached egg affair, in a range of options from your standard homemade Hollandaise to filet mignon, mushroom bordelaise sauce, Cajun chicken sausage and the ever-popular "Billy Bob Benedict," which favors fried eggs, bacon and country gravy.

The White House serves up a mighty omelet, too, with crowd favorites being the White House Omelet topped (again) in its own homemade Hollandaise (hey, this Hollandaise could be ladled on every item on the menu and I'd be happy), and Wyland's omelet, which is the artist Wyland's actual request of fillings with a side of his favorite homemade salsa.

On the weekend brunch menu, the pricing doesn't go up, but the selection expands from about 25 items to more than 60 to include waffles, French toast, breakfast burritos, salads, sandwiches, every kind of burger and even light pastas.

The servers are down-home friendly and attentive, fresh coffee is always making its rounds, and anything I order arrives quickly and piping hot. I guess after 95 years of serving Laguna customers, you might say the White House has it down!

ZINC CAFÉ & MARKET

350 Ocean Ave., Laguna Beach, CA 92651
(949) 494-6302, Market: (949) 494-2791

Breakfast, lunch, average $9 – $15
Hours: Café, 7 a.m. – 4 p.m.; Market, 7 a.m. – 6 p.m.
(Dinner is also served during high summer)
Noise level at busiest: 2 out of 10
Good for kids? Yes
Dogs: Yes

Menu: www.LagunaBeachBest.com/Menus/Zincs-Café-Laguna-Beach

Simply said, the Zinc Café & Market is a glorious find in Laguna Beach. It is one of those rare places that relaxes and coddles you the moment you step into its umbrellaed courtyard of tables and chairs.

Founded by Laguna Beach resident John Secretan in 1988, this vegetarian and organic foods devotee decided it was high time someone introduce classic, sophisticated vegetarian dishes to Laguna Beach. John's own mother is responsible for the majority of the recipes and dishes on demand; it's quite obvious this woman can do no wrong.

The café is inspired by the famous Berkeley-based Chez Panisse and its remarkable chef and owner Alice Waters. Zinc's is divided into two portions. The market side of Zinc's offers take-home and catering-style vegetarian dishes and desserts (including a revolving vertical display of the most amazing cakes and pies, good glory.) You will also find eclectic wine finds and an always-changing display of interesting decor items, serving dishes, cookbook and greeting card choices. The Café side offers a gourmet vegetarian breakfast and lunch menu (summers add a dinner menu). Both sides of Zinc's serve up Zinc's famous coffee and tea blends.

Largely a locals' hangout, Zinc's is always, always busy. While some weekend days will see the Café line of breakfast hopefuls snaking down the outside sidewalk, Zinc's late mornings and afternoons beckon you in for a generous frittata slice or a fresh-baked Snicker Doodle cookie.

At Zinc's, every dish is a healthy turn on the traditional. Take, for instance, the Huevos Rancheros, this time created with papaya salsa, black bean chili and smoked Gouda. Or, try the Burrito Bowl, a blend of eggs with vegetarian sausage, onion, leaks, tomato and cheeses. For lunch, the Café offers a variety of sandwiches (even on gluten-free bread), inventive pizzettes (try the Potato & Arugula, I kid you not), a healthy heap of inventive salads, and Vegetarian Chili that will make you Zinc's slave forever.

Zinc's is an enclave. It is a place that allows Laguna Beach residents to re-connect on an almost daily basis. I still remember the day I walked into Zinc's with my neighbors, Susie and Heather, and sat down to a table that included one of Laguna's most famous artists in paint-stained flannel shirt and ratty jeans. The dude just hangs out, incognito, with a band of retired schoolteachers, Montage Resort muckety mucks, and inventors describing their latest ventures.

There are very few places in Laguna Beach that define the soul of this rather eccentric and wonderful town … Zinc's is one of them.

Best Bars & Happy Hours

Starfish Asian Cuisine
30832 S. Coast Highway • Laguna Beach

Starfish Asian Cuisine
30832 S. Coast Highway • Laguna Beach

Note to readers: This section contains a few features on bars, live music and happy hours.

The Happy Hour Directory for Laguna Beach resides at the end of this section. The directory divides restaurants geographically into four sections: North Laguna Beach, Downtown & Restaurant Row, South Central Laguna & The H.I.P. District, and South Laguna Beach.

Because the happy hour offerings change seasonally, you can find specifics on each of these listed happy hours at www.LagunaBeachBest.com/HappyHourDirectory

STARFISH ASIAN CUISINE

Best Bartender & Best Original Cocktails

30832 S. Coast Highway, Laguna Beach, CA 92651
(949) 715-9200

Happy Hour Average $5 – 10; Opium Hour: 3:00 – 6:00 p.m. every day. Industry Night for hospitality professionals – 50% off all food and drinks Monday night

When Starfish Asian Cuisine in South Laguna Beach first opened, primary management came in from Tabu Grill to set the tone and pace. This thankfully included Master Mixologist Neil Skewes. Not only is Neil the nicest bartender I've met in Laguna Beach in the 13 years I've lived here, he's one seriously talented mixologist. Apparently, I'm not the only one who has reached this conclusion – any time I write about Neil, I hear from readers who've known him for two decades in this place or that as he worked his way up the bartending ladder.

Any time the restaurant is open, Neil's entire specialty cocktail list is available – and each is 50% off during Starfish's daily "Opium Happy Hour" (3-6 p.m.). Take a few minutes to peruse this cocktail menu, as it's quite an inventive leap from your average martini. Consider, for instance, Buddha's Kiss (pictured here) with Veev Acai Spirit, sake, house-made papaya puree in a chilled martini glass with a chili-salted rim. Or, try the Red Lotus with Prosecco, pomegranate liqueur, blood orange bitters and hibiscus syrup with a flower. The Yokohama might claim to be a martini, but with coconut vodka, lemongrass syrup and coconut water, it's a surprising taste treat combination. Narrowing it down to just one cocktail is a serious task.

When asked about his proclivity for unique cocktail creations, Neil just grins and claims years of education "on the job." Be sure to ask for his holiday specials (at Halloween and Valentine's Day, they will be the drinks that are literally smokin') and if you really can't find a single cocktail you would prefer, just give him an idea of the kind of drink you like, and let Neil work his magic.

The "Small Bites" featured in Opium Hour are always available any time of the day, but during Opium Hour, they're 50% off. On Industry Night for hospitality professionals on Mondays, the "Opium Hour" lasts all night long!

Priced in groups of $5, $7 and $9, this hearty menu of 20 or so appetizers proves highly inventive, tasty and memorable. This last year, Executive Chef Marco Romero began to add sushi rolls to the menu, and met with surprising fanfare. His Crisp Lobster Egg Rolls are so decadent I can't even begin to explain it. And, Chef Marco's Spicy Tuna Roll is my favorite "formal roll" as the ever-inventive Chef wraps in avocado, daikon, cucumber, jalapeno and fried shallots with the Ahi.

Pressed for favorites, I'd say order the Pan-Seared Pork Dumplings, the light and crispy Singapore Bamboo Roll, the Korean Galbi Tacos and the Crisp Lobster Egg Rolls.

MONTAGE LOBBY LOUNGE

30801 S. Coast Highway, Laguna Beach, CA 92651
(949) 715-6000
Hours: 6 a.m. – 1 a.m

Every Sunday morning, I pack up my book and journal and walk the sandy beach from West Street down to the Montage Resort. On arrival, I clean up my sandy feet, put on my Rainbows, grab a complimentary cup of coffee in the Loft restaurant and head up to the Montage's Lobby Lounge for a happy Sunday morning ritual I don't think I'll ever stop doing.

I know, I know. I live in Laguna Beach, and I have a home beachside just a mile down from The Montage, so why bother going to this place? Well, the way I see it, there's no better way start to my workweek than getting my mind in the right frame of mind with the "frame" of the opulent Montage Lobby around me. To my surprise, I don't see any locals here on a Sunday morning, and I wonder why. This is truly one of the most magnificent resorts in the world, right here under our noses, and the staff here is just as friendly to locals as it is to the many

visitors it welcomes from around the world.

When you first enter The Montage Laguna Beach hotel from the street, this sprawling Lobby Lounge is ... well ... breathtaking in both decor and ocean view. At the same time, though, it's extremely cozy and comfortable. To one side, you have an enormous fireplace with cushy chairs, couches and small tabletops. And to the other side, you have a massive bar stretching from one side of the room to the other. Throughout this expansive Lobby, you have more couches and sinkable chairs around low-slung tables. And, if standing in awe at the ocean-side open balcony isn't enough, you're welcome to grab a table and chairs at the patios, which sit on either side of the centerpiece balcony.

I'll often trot up to this renowned Laguna Beach hotel's Lobby Lounge in the early evening, too, before heading into Laguna Beach.

While there are any number of languages moving around this Montage Lobby at one time, and while there's really no rhyme or reason to sudden swells in thirsty patrons, the servers are sophisticated, friendly and fast. No, the drinks aren't "Happy Hour" cheap, but I've paid similar prices at other restaurants and bars in Laguna Beach that don't have anything close to the view or cosmopolitan energy of this place. While I favor the *Montage Lobby Lounge's Cucumber Cooler*, the Lounge bar reads like a small phone book –

- 20 wines by the glass,
- 22 beers from every point of the globe,
- Full, single pages devoted to vodka, whiskey and single malts
- Rum, gin, tequila, cognac (read: Hardy's Perfection at $850), brandy and port in profuse assortment
- And a large menu of specialty drinks, martinis, margaritas, etc.

With live piano music in one corner, a roaring fire in the far corner, and a wealth of some of the most interesting people you'll see and meet, it's no wonder the Montage Lobby Lounge reminds me – on a weekly basis - that I live in one of the rarest finds on Planet Earth.

MOZAMBIQUE

1740 S. Coast Highway, Laguna Beach, CA 92651
(949) 715-7777

Hours: Fri/Sat, 8:45 p.m. – midnight,
Sundays, 5:00 p.m. – 10:00 p.m.

On the second floor of Mozambique's restaurant sits its amazing bar and lounge. Although you can be served a full dinner in this bar area, you'll want to hang on to your seat any time after 9:00 on the weekends. No matter who's warming up on stage at 9:00 p.m., Mozambique's bar and adjacent dance floor fills up fast with a happily rowdy bunch of live music enthusiasts. The energy and fun in this place is contagious, and the people watching is one-of-a-kind.

Fridays and Saturdays bring in an eclectic variety of bands, with local favorite Nick I & A.D.D. (from the band, Common Sense) often showing on Friday nights for several sets of Reggae, rock and soul. National touring bands and single artists like Macy Gray, Smash Mouth and George Clinton also grace the stage.

Sundays are Reggae Sundays, and the action starts early at 5:00 p.m. with big names (Wailing Souls, Black Uhuru, etc.) as well as regional and local favorites (local-based World Anthem is a rarity, but one worth watching for in the Mozambique calendar).

Hint: Get in early for a commandeered seat at the bar (or as close as you can get to it) as it's quite a wrangle for servers to work through the crowd. I always say the closer you are to easy delivery, the better!

Sunset cruise

SANDPIPER ("THE DIRTY BIRD")

1183 S. Coast Highway, Laguna Beach, CA 92651
(949) 494-4694

Best Bar to the Bitter End

Hours: Daily, 1:00 p.m. – 2:00 a.m.

If you're into late night bars, this is THE Laguna Beach bar you just can't miss.

Open 365 days a year and run by the same family since the 1940s, the Sandpiper could very well be the most well-known Laguna Beach "landmark" ever. Whether locals readily admit it or not, there are probably less than five adult residents here in Laguna who have NOT stepped foot in the Sandpiper at some point in their tenure here.

Part of what I call the "Triumvirate" of Bars in Laguna Beach, the Sandpiper sits on the south side of Laguna Beach and is usually the last of the bars to close its doors in the wee morning hours. Locals, in fact, joke that the Sandpiper takes in all the folks who "roll downhill" from every other late night bar in Laguna (primarily Ocean Brewery, The Marine Room, The White House, The Saloon and Mozambique).

'Round about 12:30 a.m., you'll see partiers converge from all sides for stiff pours, live music and loud conversation.

The Dirty Bird has been eternally owned by the Harrell family, with Chuck, his brothers and his mom, Jeana, taking turns at the bar. To this day, and just about every night of the week, you'll see Chuck in the middle of it all, happily pouring drinks, and participating in a number of conversations at once.

Live music happens most evenings, with Reggae and top 40s blends usually trading nights. The dance floor is crammed and active, and people are lined up for pool tables and dartboards in the back as well. As the late-night hours progress, you're going to find it wall-to-wall people on weekend evenings and just about every evening of the week during our summer months. Wade in with a smile.

Best Hangover Cure?

There's nothing finer than Laguna Feast's smothered breakfast burrito (see *Breakfasts*), but if you prefer that "hair of the dog" routine, try the Build-Your-Own Bloody Mary bar at the Lumberyard Restaurant for Sunday brunch.

SPLASHES AT THE SURF & SAND RESORT

1555 S. Coast Highway, Laguna Beach, CA 92651
(949) 376-2779

Hours at the Splashes bar: All week, 11 a.m. – 11 p.m.

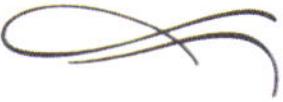

I love the fact that our top-tier hotel resorts in Laguna always welcome locals. And, I love the fact that David Fune, the Executive Chef of Splashes at the Surf and Sand Resort, rides a big motorcycle to and from work.

Since his arrival to Splashes, Fune has added a very innovative, fresh flair to what many in the food industry would have called "a plate of browns." His style extends easily to the famous Splashes bar, which perches on the north side of the restaurant directly on the beach. I mean DIRECTLY on the beach. You can't get any closer to the rolling surf than at Splashes, and with the bar windows open, you'll often feel the fine mist of the waves as they roll in.

A food truck aficionado, Fune has brought some fun to the Splashes menu with Baked Mac 'n Cheese served up differently every week, fabulous Fish Tacos, Hangover Nachos, Tartufo Fries with garlic and smoky blue cheese crème, and his famous Pork Belly and Coffee-Dijon Chicken Burgers.

It's a great menu in one of the most unforgettable perches in Laguna Beach. Make sure you don't miss it.

Best Live Music on a Sunday Afternoon "Sunday Service"

THE MARINE ROOM

214 Ocean Ave., Laguna Beach, CA 92651
(949) 494-3027

Hours: Weekdays, 10:00 a.m. – last call;
Weekends, 10:00 a.m. – 2:00 a.m.

Yesterday (Sunday), I spent a great afternoon and evening hanging with one of my coolest girlfriends and her boyfriend, Billy, who just happens to be turning FIFTY-FIVE today. (Happy Birthday toooo yooou ... you don't look a day over 21, dear man.)

Because Billy is a seriously accomplished drummer in the L.A.-and-beyond world, and because he and my GF used to be residents here, there was really no other option than to begin the festivities at our famous Laguna Beach Sunday Service.

That's right. This Sunday Service has been going on for 20 years and residents here attend religiously, let me tell you.

It's the Marine Room Tavern's weekly live band, Missiles of October, from just 4 – 8 p.m. Seriously, these boys have rarely missed doing this famous Sunday Service for 20 STRAIGHT years.

Now, I've written about the Marine Room before – it's one of just three "bars" in Laguna Beach. I call it the "Triumvirate," a veritable and powerful benevolent regime of the three only existing bars in Laguna Beach. (We sadly lost Woody's and The Boom Boom Room in recent years.)

1. We have the Marine Room Tavern across from Main Beach in Laguna Beach …
2. The infamous Saloon just two blocks up PCH from the Marine Room, the only Southern California stand up bar …
3. And we have the Sandpiper (aka: The Dirty Bird) heading toward the south of Laguna Beach.

It's the Marine Room that brings in the majority of bikers, especially in summer months, and it's always a roaring good time. (And the people watching is QUITE extraordinary.) You will see a bunch of black leather in every possible clothing option, but this is by no means a nasty biker's hangout. While the Marine caters to middle-age folks, you'll see tables of 20-somethings next to tables of 50-somethings, all getting along quite amicably.

As for our famous Laguna Beach Sunday Service here … well, there's nothing like it in the OC as live music goes. The Missiles are a critically acclaimed, highly talented band, singing classic covers and a lot of their own great tunes. Poul Pedersen, the lead singer and founder of the band was in the Breeze Brothers in Santa Barbara back in the '70s, and his cronies Frank Cotinola (drums), Jimmy Perez (bass), and Richard Bredice (lead guitar) weren't far behind. Missiles itself has been together for years and years and that's something to be said in and of itself.

photo credit: The Marine Room

Locals and tourists alike crowd into the tiny dance floor (about the size of a coffin) and dance between tables. If they can't fit in the doors, they hang on the open windowsills from the sidewalk and do their swing steps there on the concrete.

The Missiles of October just deliver that kind of vibe. The bar serves everything from classic roadhouse to top shelf, the servers are cool and the prices are reasonable.

So, next time you're feeling like some glory and hallelujah, we're not telling you to skip your morning Sunday Service. Just come on down to the afternoon's follow-up to stay in the proper, joyful vibe all the daylong.

ROOFTOP LOUNGE

1289 S. Coast Highway (top of La Casa del Camino Hotel), Laguna Beach, CA 92651
Reservations only taken for parties of 6 or more (for a fee): (949) 497-2446

Happy Hour pricing: $6 – 10
Happy Hours: 3:00 – 5:00 p.m.

This week, our little Laguna Beach town has happily climbed in temp from low 60s to today's 78 degrees. I'm sitting up here in my condo, looking down at a beach half-packed with people and wondering if anyone works on Fridays anymore.

So, this will be a short post as I'm off to Happy Hour with friends at Laguna Beach's popular happy hour watering hole in town – the Rooftop.

Granted, we locals usually stay away from this "see and be seen" hotel rooftop bar on Fridays and weekends, but you've got to celebrate the coming of summer SOME time, and today seems to be that day.

Seriously, how many places can you get a view like this at happy hour anywhere in Southern Cal? Laguna Beach's Rooftop restaurant sits on top of the Casa del Camino hotel at PCH and Cress. Owned by the same gentlemen who own one of my favorites, K'ya down below, the Rooftop serves up the same great food, but in a smaller menu that proves "heartier" in fare. (Every dish must be trotted up several flights of stairs, so you can't be ordering stuff like K'ya's famous lobster mac and cheese dish.) You still have plenty of snacking with sandwiches, huge salads, and unique appetizers.

Clambered to by many a celebrity and celebrity athlete, the Rooftop puts on quite a show of peeps at times, especially between 7:30 and its closing bell at 10:00. The Rooftop Happy Hour starts the evening early with 3:00 - 5:00 p.m. half-off specials on all Mojitos, beer, wine and well drinks.

I'm skeedaddling out the door ... don't want to miss the sunset, of course. See you at the Rooftop one of these eves!

Life in Laguna Beach

Powered paragliders cruise Laguna's beautiful coastline.

THE SALOON

446 S. Coast Highway, Laguna Beach, CA 92651
(949) 494-5469

Hours: Weekdays, 2:00 p.m. to last call; Weekends, noon to last call (usually 1:30 a.m. All drinks are out of hands and off the bar at 2:00 a.m.)

Granted, there are a number of great restaurant bars in Laguna Beach (i.e., Rooftop, K'ya, Lumberyard, The White House, Nick's, 230 Forest, etc.) but there are only three REAL bars in Laguna Beach, all with personalities of their own.

Together, these three long-standing Laguna Beach bars are a veritable triumvirate in our little town, having dominated and outlasted hundreds of other tries over the decades. They are: The Marine Room Tavern (Ocean Ave.), the Saloon (PCH right in the middle of town), and The Sandpiper Lounge (PCH toward the south end of Central Laguna).

Today, we discuss the Saloon, the only standup European pub in the entirety of Orange County.

Established in 1978, Laguna Beach's Saloon has been owned these last five years by Bobby Doerr and Mike Byrne. Step in the place and you feel you've been immediately transported to some pub in Central London or Dublin. Aside from a couple of small benches and one teensy table in the corner, this is a stand-up bar. Don't be asking for one of those foo-foo blender drinks – they don't own a blender. DO feel free to peruse one of the finest single Scotch menus in town, and enjoy 100% juice in any mixed juice drink you try – they refuse to go the way of "juice from a gun."

While the Saloon certainly offers above-average wines by the glass, this is primarily a mixed drinks, straight shots, and mighty beer kind of bar.

The Saloon opens its doors at noon on weekends and at 2:00 on weekdays, but the real action begins after 9:00 p.m. Packed with locals, nearby town regulars and people who come from all cities and countries to this renowned bar, just take a deep breath and worm your way through. (Come on, that's half the fun.)

Local, Insider Tips to the Saloon

The Saloon is famous for two drinks:

1. **The Pine-O Cranikazi.** See that big ol' jug of fresh-cut pineapple rings soaking in vodka there on the Saloon's back bar? That's the foundation to this drink. It's a pineapple-infused top-shelf vodka Cosmopolitan served up or on the rocks, it goes down extremely easy.
2. **The No Name shot.** Primarily a coffee liqueurs shot, this gizmo was first invented by a Filipino bartender at the Saloon years ago and was initially named after him. When he eventually retired, the shot became the "NO Name" shot. This either occurred because of some kind of strange politics OR a reverence for retiring the name, much like they do a Michael Jordan jersey number. (I prefer the latter story.) Whatever the case, this is a no-nonsense shot made up of 5 liquors (yes, FIVE) and mixed on a weekly basis by just one, long-time bartender at the Saloon. If you know the actual name of the shot, the Saloon treats you like a V.I.P. You'll see the clear, unnamed, unlabeled bottle there on the back bar, too.

230 FOREST

230 Forest Ave., Laguna Beach, CA 92651
(949) 494-2545

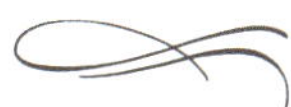

Because Laguna Beach is a sophisticated party town, we have more than our share of tremendously talented bartenders. That being said, you don't want to miss "Dan the Man's" martini-making abilities at one of Laguna Beach's favorite restaurants, 230 Forest.

Dan Vincent has been at his craft for more than 30 years, but when it comes to his famous martnis, this isn't just a craftsman you're dealing with here – this is a genius. Yes, the ingredients going in the shaker all LOOK like the same sort of ingredients you'd see going in any bartender's martini shaker, but what pours from Dan's shaker is hardly run-of-the-mill or ordinary.

Dan was one of the first hires at 230 Forest when it opened its doors 20 years ago, and having Dan the Man overseeing your libations is a very big plus. He's most renowned for his Lemon Drop martini. It's not on the menu, per se, but ask for it anyway (we locals do without hesitation).

WHITE HOUSE RESTAURANT & NIGHTCLUB

340 S. Coast Highway, Laguna Beach, CA 92651
(949) 494-8088

Hours: 8:00 p.m. – 2:00 a.m.

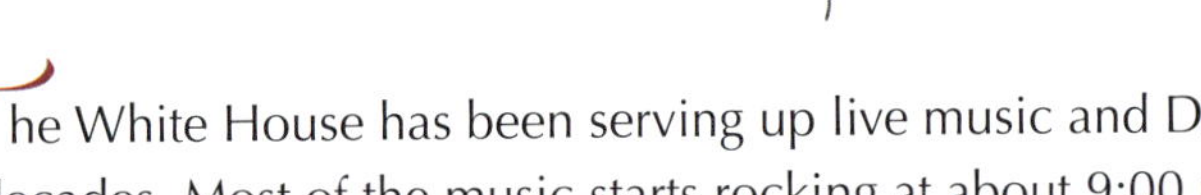

The White House has been serving up live music and DJs for decades. Most of the music starts rocking at about 9:00 p.m., and the inviting dance floor is certainly one of the largest in Laguna Beach. The White House offers retro and hip-hop through its DJs, and primarily specializes in bringing in great live rock and reggae bands.

Drinks at the White House run the gamut and are strong pours (fair warning). Be sure to ask for Jason's margarita (picured above) as it's one of the best in all of Laguna Beach (see *Best Margaritas*, next page).

Best Nightclubs/ Dance Bars

BRUSSELS BISTRO

222 Forest Ave., Laguna Beach, CA 92651
(949) 376-7955
Hours: 10:00 pm. – 2:00 a.m.

Every Saturday evening at 10:30 p.m., Brussels Bistro's tabled tavern transforms to a dance floor with DJs in the house. Featuring "Euro electric music," DJs spin an eclectic mix to a crowd of the same ilk. Its a fun and engaging way to feel like you've jetted off to Europe without the cramped airplane seat.

CLUB BOUNCE AT CLUB MAIN STREET

1460 S. Coast Highway, Laguna Beach, CA 92651
(949) 494-0056
Hours: 2:00 p.m. – 2:00 a.m.

The last gay bar standing in Laguna Beach, Main Street proffers great drinks, fun bartenders and a gay and lesbian audience that welcomes anyone of any stripe. Club Bounce is the officially named dance floor, and it's a busy one any night of the week. Music ranges from '70s to recent top 40s, techno, deep house and electronic.

Best Margaritas in Laguna Beach – The Top 6

photo credit: Diane Alms

Here's how the search for the best margaritas began … I polled my thousands of readers, and they told me where to go. I then faithfully donated my gall bladder to science in an effort to taste test their votes.

In the last week, I had 46 comments arrive with votes for Coyote Grill (tried it), 230 Forest (tried it), Nick's (tried it), K'ya (tried it), the Lumberyard (scheduled for tomorrow), the Saloon (haven't gotten there yet), and Sapphire (tried it, the most expensive on the list).

For the record, this is such intensive testing that I'm doing no more than a few sips per drink. If I were downing all of these, I'd be sick as a dog, assuredly. My personal trainer, Craig Hartley, however, is still appalled that I've taken up this subject of research at all, and insists we include Skinny Margaritas on the list.

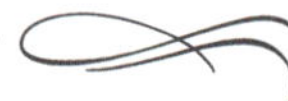

1. **The Partida, Carmelita's**
   217 Broadway, Laguna Beach, CA 92651
   (949) 715-7829

Photo credit: Diane Alms

All of the margaritas at Carmelita's are basically "skinny" as Carmelita's only uses agave and fresh juices. While the Carmelita's Grilled Pineapple Margarita (actually pictured here) is a crowd favorite, I was first recommended the Partida Marg with anejo tequila. It was so spectacular that I've had difficulty choosing any other on the Carmelita's list. It might have been the best margarita I've had yet in Laguna Beach. (Of course, every margarita at Carmelita's uses 2 shots of tequila … maybe that's why their margaritas are such crowd pleasers.)

2. **Jason's Double, The White House**
   340 S. Coast Highway, Laguna Beach, CA 92651
   (949) 494-8088

Ask for Jason's double concoction margarita at The White House. Ask only for Jason. I happened upon this Margarita Master when I was doing my Taco Tuesday story on the White House a couple years ago. He'll toss in the tequila of your choice, but favors orange juice to sweet-n-sour mix, and throws in a couple citrus extras he'll never mention by name.

3. **The Cucumber Cilantro, Carmelita's**
   217 Broadway, Laguna Beach, CA 92651
   (949) 715-7829

Yep, I've listed Carmelita's again, this time for its very cool and refreshing cucumber/cilantro margarita. Again made with two shots of silver tequila and a muddle of cucumber slices with chopped cilantro, this goes down terribly easy on a hot summer afternoon.

4. The 363 Margarita, Ocean View Bar & Grill

Hotel Laguna
425 S. Coast Highway, Laguna Beach, CA 92651
(949) 494-1151

Tucked back behind the Hotel Laguna right in the heart of Laguna Beach downtown is the lovely Ocean View Bar & Grill restaurant. When the sun is shining and the dolphins are playing, there are few better places in all of Laguna to sit for a spell and sip a great margarita. The Grill's "363 Margarita" is the bomb because, instead of common skimps on tequila in lesser margaritas, the Grill brings you your own bottle.

Each margarita comes ready-made minus the tequila. That's what your accompanying mini bottle of Patron Tequila is for.

Add the entire bottle, or toss in dashes in the name of moderation; it's entirely up to you. (But, please, for a great tasting margarita, DO toss in the tequila. The waitresses tell me that many people will suck down the margarita mix in the glass without realizing the tequila hasn't been added.)

5. The Skinny, Avila's El Ranchito

1305 S. Coast Highway, Laguna Beach, CA 92651
(949) 376-7040

Actually, a number of you folks mentioned skinny margaritas in your votes, and I'm all for a healthier alternative. El Ranchito's Skinny Margarita, concocted largely with lime juice and a splash of soda, is quite refreshing and not at all gummy as some margaritas can be.

6. Jalapeno Margarita, K'ya and The Rooftop

1287 S. Coast Highway, Laguna Beach, CA 92651
(949) 376-9718

When many readers began steering me to the K'ya Jalapeno Margarita, I thought I was reading some sort of group hallucination typo.

This is one brash, take-no-prisoners kind of hombre. The folks muddle Casa Nobles Organic tequila with fresh jalapeno, lime, lemon and orange slices. They toss in Cointreau and Organic Agave Nectar, shake it with ice, and serve it up with lime and jalapeno slices in a glass rimmed in chili and lime spices.

It starts off tasting like a darned good sippin' margarita, and then sneaks up and wallops you a good one. It's served up in both K'ya downstairs in the Casa del Camino, and at the Rooftop Lounge, same location.

RESTAURANTS & BARS THAT OFFER HAPPY HOURS IN LAGUNA BEACH

The Happy Hours in Laguna Beach are divided according to the section of town in which they reside. Please note that participation and hours can randomly change in the chart below. Go to LagunaBeachBest.com/HappyHours for complete details on what's being served where.

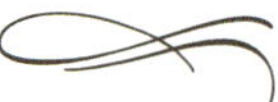

North Laguna Beach to Broadway

Gina's Pizza	610 N. Coast Highway, #106	3-6 p.m. M-F

Downtown Laguna Beach & Restaurant Row

Big Fish Tavern	540 S. Coast Hwy #200	4-6 p.m. M-F, bar only
Brussels Bistro	222 Forest Ave.	3-6:30 p.m. daily
Carmelita's	217 Broadway St.	4-6 p.m. daily
C'est la Vie	373 S. Coast Highway	3:30-6 p.m. M-F
Cliff Restaurant	577 S. Coast Highway	4-1 p.m. M-Th
GG's Bistro	540 S. Coast Hwy #108	4-6 p.m. M-F
Henessey's Tavern	213 Ocean Ave.	4-7 p.m. M-F
Lumberyard Restaurant	384 Forest Ave.	3:30-6:30 p.m. M-F bar and patio
Mare Culinary Lounge	696 S. Coast Highway	4-6 p.m. + 9 p.m.-close, daily
The Marine Room	214 Ocean Ave.	3:30-6:30 p.m. daily
Nirvana Grille & Bliss Bar	303 Broadway St.	5 p.m.-close T-Sun
Ocean Avenue Brewery	237 Ocean Ave.	3-6 p.m. M-F
Pizza Lounge	397 S. Coast Highway	3-6 p.m. M-F
Rockin Fish	422 S. Coast Highway	4-6 p.m., daily, bar and lounge only
Romeo Cucina	249 Broadway	4-7 p.m. M-F, bar only

The Deck at Pacific Edge	627 Sleepy Hollow Lane	3-6 p.m. M-F
The Saloon	46 S. Coast Highway	4-7 p.m. daily
Three Seventy Common	370 Glenneyre St.	4-6 p.m. M-F, bar only
Tommy Bahama's Restaurant	400 S. Coast Highway	3-6 p.m. M-F, bar only
Watermarc	448 S. Coast Highway	4-6 p.m. M-F, bar only
The White House	340 S. Coast Highway	3-6 p.m. M-F

South Central Laguna & The Hip District

Club Main Street & Club Bounce	1460 S. Coast Highway	2-8 p.m. daily
Dizz's As Is	2795 S. Coast Highway	5-7 p.m. T-Su, bar
El Ranchito	1305 S. Coast Highway	3-6 p.m. M-F
Gina's Pizza	1100 S. Coast Highway	3-6 p.m. M-F
K'Ya Bistro	1287 S. Coast Highway	4:30-5:30 p.m. daily, all night Tuesdays
Mozambique	1740 S. Coast Highway	4-6 p.m. M-F
Rooftop Lounge	1289 S. Coast Highway	3-5 p.m. M-F
Selanne Steak Tavern	1464 S. Coast Highway	5 – 7 p.m. T-Su, bar

South Laguna Beach

Coyote Grill	31621 S. Coast Highway	3-6:30 p.m. daily, bar only
Starfish Asian Coastal Cuisine	30832 S. Coast Highway	4-6 p.m. Su-F + 10 p.m.- midnight, F/S
Tabu Grill	2892 S. Coast Highway	5:30–6:30 p.m., bar only and all evening on patio, Su & Tu-Th

Best Snacks & Desserts

Starfish Asian Cuisine
30832 Pacific Coast Highway • Laguna Beach

ANDREE'S PATISSERIE

1456 S. Coast Highway, Laguna Beach, CA 92651
(949) 494-1577

Pastry average: $2 – $4
Hours: Mondays, 7:35 a.m. – noon Tuesday – Friday, 7:35 a.m. – 3:00 p.m. Saturday, 7:35 a.m. – 1:00 p.m. Closed Sunday
Noise level at busiest: 2 out of 10
Good for kids? Yes
Dogs: No

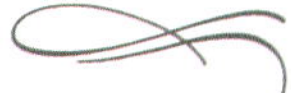

After 32 years as the owner of Andree's Patisserie, and after 41 years of baking pastries, you can bet that Ron Reno knows how to make a great cinnamon roll. Apparently, thousands of fans believe he has this art down, as they are diehard fans of the oversized, super fresh creations. Granted, this man creates more than 100 unbelievable pastries of at least 12 different kinds every single weekday, but his Cinnamon Rolls seem to receive particular fanfare. You're not going to get a day-old cinnamon roll here, oh no. Each and every morning (except Sunday), Ron Reno rolls out of bed at about 4:00 a.m. to ensure that his new and repeat clients receive piping hot, fresh baked goods across the board. While his Scones, Chocolate Croissants, Bear Claws and enormous Elephant Ears are also great sellers, his Cinnamon Rolls are normally some of the first to clear out. Get there early (he opens at 7:35 a.m.) or be relegated to sad crumbs.

BONZAI BOWLS

1100 S. Coast Highway, Laguna Beach, CA 92651
(949) 715-8989

Hours: 8:00 a.m. – 6:00 p.m.
Noise level at busiest: 4 out of 10
Good for kids? Yes
Dogs: No

First in Costa Mesa, Bonzai Bowls quietly made its way into Laguna Beach a few years ago, and it's been nothing less than a constant stream of human "ants" in and out the doors ever since. (Especially high school human ants – they love this place.)

With a base of healthy berry Acai, the folks at Bonzai whip up a veritable mountain of fresh, organic, fruits, nuts, milks, and even spinach and celery to create any one of six smoothies or seven acai bowls. No sugars, yogurt, sorbet or ice.

Each starts with a blend of juice and fresh fruit, and then a mound of toppings is loaded up. As an example, one of their best sellers, the Shark's Cove, blends apple juice or soy milk with acai, bananas and strawberries, and tops it all off with granola, more strawberries, bananas, blueberries, and Goji berries. It's a large plastic beer cup of fabulous, healthy goodness.

For me, I prefer their SMALL Maui edition (a heaping helping of coconut milk and pineapple juice with strawberries, mango, coconut shreds, bananas and blueberries.) Without a doubt, Bonzai deserves its namesake.

CHOCOLATE SOLDIER

1200 S. Coast Highway (in the old Pottery Shack complex),
Laguna Beach, CA 92651
(949) 494-4462

Hours: 8:00 a.m. – 6:00 p.m.

Time to focus on what's truly important in life – the best, daily-made chocolate decadence this side of the Mississippi …

A Laguna Beach resident since 1967, De Francis is the 25-year owner of The Chocolate Soldier, with shops located in the Dana Point Harbor and The Old Pottery Place in the HIP District.

As many of our life paths unfold, De never suspected she would end up being a chocolatier. In the waning 1970s, when interest rates soared and the real estate market slowed to a crawl, De Francis hung up her broker's license and did what every other panicking real estate agent should have done – she got a job surrounded in chocolate.

"How can you not be happy with chocolate in your life?" she asks. (A rhetorical question, for sure.)

Continuing a 145-Year Tradition

Chocolate making is really pretty basic, says De. You have three types of chocolate – milk, white and dark. You have five different nuts. And you have about 10 popular fruit, liqueur and caramel fillings.

De only uses Guittard Chocolate, the 145-year premium chocolate first introduced by Etienne Guittard, who emigrated from France to San Francisco in 1868 in hopes of trading chocolate for mining supplies. (Fortunately, the miners refused to trade their supplies, instead insisting on more chocolate.)

By far the best seller, The Chocolate Soldier's Toffee is consistently voted *The Best of Orange County*. (Small wonder as its 4 pounds of butter rivals the same amount of sugar swirled in.)

De figures that the Black Satin Meltaway is the shop's second best seller. "It's dark chocolate all the way through," she quips. She and her compadres create 12 or more different Meltaways, each of which features a blend of chocolates with a low melting temperature to create the creamy soft innards.

Truffles are the next best seller, with the All Dark Truffle again taking the lead. "Truffles are the Cadillac of chocolates," says De.

The team creates more than 20 different truffles, each filled with anything from fruit puree and fruit cream centers to champagne or Chambord.

De's favorite in the bunch? "Well, I love caramel," she says. "In fact, let's try a Sea Salt Caramel right now ... You really need to have caramel in your diet every day."

DOLCE GELATO

247 Broadway Street, Laguna Beach, CA 92651
(949) 715-9249

Hours: Sunday – Thursday, noon – 10 p.m.;
Friday and Saturday, noon – 11 p.m.
Noise level at busiest: 1 out of 10
Good for kids? Yes
Dogs: No

There's nothing like Dolce Gelato in the world, and it is the only one in the world. Owners Rick and Claudia Baedeker opened the shop in May 2010, based entirely on Rick's love of making homemade ice cream for his family. Now, son Danny runs the show.

Rick's short-term plan for their gelato store involved creating hundreds of flavors, with new flavors featured every week. And now, just a few years later, Dolce Gelato has more than 300 homegrown recipes and features 33 flavors of sorbet and gelato every single day.

"We go through at least a pan every day on every flavor, so we're spending a little more than eight hours a day making gelato just for our shop. And then we start in on our restaurant orders," quips Danny as he trots back to the big gelato machine just in time to catch more emerging frozen goodness.

Gelato-making is a two-part process, but that process is done two different ways. Rick attended "gelato school" in New York, and learned how to make gelato the way most shops in the U.S. do – create a foundational base, cook it, and then fold in flavoring during the freezing process.

When Rick started turning out initial batches, though, he wasn't pleased with the depth of flavor. So, the family made two genius decisions.

First, they sought out the "queen of gelato," Italian American Maria Coassin, Owner of Seattle's famous Gelatiamo. In an exclusive agreement, she agreed to teach them how to make Italian gelato, and worked side-by-side with them until they had it perfected.

Instead of creating a base with folded flavors, Coassin's old school method insists on creating one gelato recipe as a whole, thereby adjusting and blending appropriately for the added fruits, vegetables and juices. The recipe is cooked (who knew gelato was cooked?) and frozen in one meandering, melding process. Then, the gelato machine is completely sluiced with water and the next recipe begins.

Then, the Baedekers brought on Gelato Chef Lindsey Nelson. (Hey, if you're going to create three new flavors of gelato every single week, you have to bring in the big guns.) "Lindsey is the most creative person I've every worked with," says Rick. "For Lindsey, gelato making is an adventure, and she loves the challenge of coming up with our amazing flavors.

Apparently, Dolce Gelato's growing line of admirers feels the same. The shop's consistent bestseller was initially one of Lindsey's weekly specials.

"Coming up with three new flavors each week really gives me an opportunity to try all sorts of ideas," says Lindsey. "So, one week in the fall a couple years ago I tried Salted Maple Caramel, and it's been our crazy seller, every single day since."

While Chocolate, Coconut and Pistachio are all consistently great sellers, Dolce Gelato serves up an unbelievable number of Crème Brûlée, Marscarpone (Italian cheese), Raspberry Chambord and Strawberry Balsamic orders.

Lindsey's Chocolate Habanero gelato has nearly topped regular Chocolate orders, and her version of "Teddy Grahams" with Muscovado brown sugar, honey and spices disappears about as quickly as the pan is put in play. Then there are the "herb" gelatos – Fresh Mint, Fresh Basil, Fresh Sage ... the creativity is endless.

On the sorbet side, Dolce Gelato offers "regular" and "non-fat" with favorites being Grapefruit Hibiscus, Strawberry Mango Lime and Arnold Palmer. If you're not a dairy person, you can also try Lindsey's almond milk creations (chocolate still the best seller there).

Feeling more decadent? Dolce bakes its own waffle cones each morning from a family recipe, but if you're going after baked goods, you simply cannot pass on the homemade cobblers, compliments of Claudia Baedeker.

The single-serving cobblers joined the party about a year and a half ago and, depending on the seasonal demand, the shop's convection oven is busy every morning with new cobbler batches of Peach Raspberry (my favorite), Blackberry, Strawberry/Rhubarb, Blueberry/Coconut and Chocolate Lava Cakes. The cobbler is served warm with your option to add any gelato scoop of your choice.

LAGUNA COFFEE COMPANY

Best Cookies

1050 S. Coast Highway, Laguna Beach, CA 92651
(949) 494-6901
Hours: Mon – Wed 6 a.m. – 6 p.m.; Thurs/Fri 6 a.m. – 8 p.m.; Sat 6:30 a.m. – 8 p.m.; Sun 7 a.m. – 6 p.m.
Noise level at busiest: 1 out of 10 on patio, 5 out of 10 inside
Good for kids? Yes
Dogs: Yes
Wi-Fi: Yes

On my way back to work after lunch today, I stopped in to pick up a quick coffee at Laguna Coffee ... and there they were ... those awesome, amazing, terrible, addicting hand-baked, secret recipe cookies that former Laguna Coffee owner, Sylvan, cooks up in his own kitchen.

Now, Sylvan is a character and style all his own and I'll probably just write a blog entry about HIM one of these days. A master French chef all his adult life, every resident in town owes at least 4 pounds of unwanted body poundage directly to Sylvan's fare. It's all his fault.

Sylvan's Famous Cookies

Sylvan is forever dreaming up – and then baking – morning pastries, paninis, and cookies, all original recipes. His two trademark cookies show up whenever he feels like having them show up and you've got to be fast – they disappear almost as quickly as they hit the little cookie cabinet there in Laguna Coffee.

His Beachcomber cookie is my favorite and, well, yes ... you could say it's healthy for you ... it's a combo of 2 kinds of chocolate, walnuts, oatmeal, raisins and whatever else he feels like chucking in the mixing bowl. Sadly, those puppies had already cleared out by my early afternoon drive-by. I was, however, lucky to find two of his Espresso Chocolate cookies still shouldered together. These cookies are a sophisticated blend of dark chocolate and espresso, and that's really all they need to say about themselves.

These are hefty cookies, so I actually ate half of my cookie and committed to saving the other half for another day. (I trot to my refrigerator often, though, to gaze at it longingly.)

So, if you're lucky enough to actually see Sylvan's Beachcomber or Espresso cookies in stock at Laguna Coffee, don't even ask your hips or thighs their opinion. This is rare foodie fare in Laguna Beach and you deserve to be a part of the privileged few who actually get its hands on these gems.

Best Carrot Cake

Kevin Montoya's Baked Goods

Hard to believe that a tiny coffee shop can house two of the best desserts in town, but these imports from Kevin Montoya's bakery, Carley Cakes, simply cannot be denied an entry. (In fact, Kevin also supplies a few of his desserts to Eva's Caribbean Kitchen, too.

Kevin is this 30-something dude who was so convinced of his calling that he skipped the usual college route to enroll and graduate from the San Francisco Baking Institute. Shortly thereafter, a friend of his – Carley Eissman – passed away from epilepsy and her mother stepped in to help Kevin get his baking business off the ground. With every sale of his decadent cakes and pastries, Kevin donates 2% of his profits to an epilepsy foundation.

THAT foundation must be one very happy charity because Kevin's baked goods last about three and a half minutes in any given location. At Laguna Coffee alone, he supplies entire, towering Carrot Cakes and Chocolate Cakes, and provides the coffee shop's best-selling Raspberry Muffins, too.

I've tried them all and I will tell you squarely – Kevin has a gift. We figure he has to be channeling some great aunt with chubby cheeks and an always-hot kitchen from an oven that's studiously on the job. When pressed, most folks will vote for his Carrot Cake slices (and now, the same Carrot Cake recipe shows up in cream cheese frosting-topped cupcakes. Good glory, he's out to take us all down.) But, whatever your fancy – chocolate, carrot or raspberry – make sure you swing by Laguna Coffee whenever you feel it's time to vastly improve your work day. Kevin's baked goods will not disappoint.

THE LOFT, MONTAGE RESORT

4th floor, 30801 S. Coast Highway, Laguna Beach, CA 92651
(949) 715-6420
Hours: 6:00 a.m. until the last one is sold

I have a confession to make.

Thanks to the Montage Resort, I've made an addict of my dearly beloved and only brother, Rob.

He can't get enough of Pastry Chef Lee Smith's Almond Croissants. It's a good thing, actually that my brother lives in Oregon or he'd be the size of a walrus.

Still, I've found myself feeding his addiction, even overnighting Almond Croissants to my entire family for Christmas Day breakfast. While they all

sent thank yous, I'm quite sure that my brother gobbled all 8 croissants between waving goodbye to the Fed Ex man in the driveway and arriving in his kitchen, telltale whiffs of powdered sugar undoubtedly on his shirt and Sorrels.

If you're going to have an addiction in life, it might as well be the Montage Almond Croissants. To begin with, these are giant edifices. They are composed of at least 4,000 sheets of phyllo pastry, 12 pounds of melted butter between each phyllo sheet, and a gallon of the richest, homemade almond filling imaginable.

I have people tell me that I really ought to try the Chocolate Croissants, too. What chocolate croissants? Once you've had one Montage Almond Croissant, you can see no other. It's like witchcraft or something.

Find these croissants in the Montage Loft Restaurant at the entry's Bistro Bar. If they've already been inhaled in this location, there's usually a secret stash to be pilfered down at the Mosaic Restaurant, the outdoor patio restaurant that sits next to the pool. Try not to drool or gibber as you make your way to either location.

PIZZA LOUNGE

397 S. Coast Highway, Laguna Beach, CA 92651
(949) 497-2277

Hours: 10 a.m. – 10 p.m.
Noise level at busiest: 5 out of 10 inside
Good for kids? Yes
Dogs: No

As a great pizza place with inventive pizzas and fantastic salads, Gary Decker's Pizza Lounge was one of my most surprising finds in Laguna Beach. I've written a more detailed entry about his standard offerings (see *Casual Dining*), but THIS is about one thing that's NOT on the menu that you have to ask for anyway.

The Pizza Lounge in Laguna Beach sports a few cool desserts (3 of which are dessert pizzas), but the one dessert item not on its printed menu – a homemade cookie ice cream sandwich. These aren't your average, ordinary, freezer-burned ice cream sandwiches.

Each day, the Pizza Lounge bakes up a fresh batch of big, chewy chocolate chip cookies, and only assembles the decadent mile-high stack stuffed with gourmet vanilla bean ice cream once you've placed your order. It is fantastic.

Desserts Mentioned in This Book's Reviews

Here are dessert reminders from dining entries previously noted in this book …

The Broadway by Amar Santana

328 Glenneyre St., Laguna Beach, CA 92651
Reservations recommended: (949) 715-8234

Photo credit: Doug Gifford

Broadway Panna Cotta

It's hard to explain what looks like a very simple dish here. For starters, this "dish" is about the size of a trough. Chef Amar's Vanilla Panna Cotta that resides inside is nearly an inch thick, and it is absolutely melt-in-your-mouth sublime love. It arrives adorned with strawberry sorbet, fresh strawberries, mint slivers and "chocolate pearls (also made in house). People actually begin to babble incoherently when they have their first spoonful, and I've witnessed GROWN people in SUITS running their fingers inside the bowl for any possible last remnants.

Café Zoolu

860 Glenneyre St., Laguna Beach, CA 92651
Reservations HIGHLY recommended and well in advance:
(949) 494-6825

"Expresso" Crème Brulée

A velvety, rich crème brulée with just the right touch of espresso mixed in, topped with mint, raspberries and a chocolate bar wafer.

K'ya Bistro

1287 S. Coast Highway,
Laguna Beach, CA 92651
(949) 376-9718

Banana Pecan Bread Pudding

Chef Craig created this Polynesian-twist classic during his Hawaiian Plantation restaurant days in Las Vegas. Thankfully, the recipe made the traveling squad when he moved to Laguna Beach. This bread "pudding" is a far cry from the gooey, gloppy bread pudding you might be more familiar with. Granted, it's every bit as rich in flavor, but it's got great density and depth. This banana pecan "bread" is freshly baked and soaked daily in its caramel bourbon sauce. Then, just before serving, it's drizzled with even more sauce and served up with rich vanilla ice cream.

Lumberyard

384 Forest Ave., Laguna Beach, CA 92651
(949) 715-3900

Hog Heaven Pie

A cookie crumb crust is probably the most docile of the ingredients here. Loaded into the crust is freshly made chocolate ganache, a layer of light-as-air peanut butter mousse, and topped with fresh whipped cream.

Maro Wood Grill

1915 S. Coast Highway, Laguna Beach, CA 92651
(949) 793-4044

The Golden Foodie Award winner for her desserts two years in a row, Chef Debra's award-winning Dark Horse Dessert consists of chocolate dulce de leche, crème anglaise, fresh raspberries, caramel sauce and chocolate sauce topped with Laguna Coffee ice cream and a homemade, chocolate-dipped honeycomb.

Ristorante Rumari

1826 S. Coast Highway, Laguna Beach, CA 92651
Reservations recommended: (949) 494-0400

Semi Freddo

Rumari's version of a hot fudge sundae, this vast improvement on the subject proffers vanilla bean and white chocolate chip ice cream with a shot of hot fudge, a shot of espresso and a crumbled amaretto cookie to top the torture.

Starfish Asian Cuisine

30832 S. Coast Highway, Laguna Beach, CA 92651
(949) 715-9200

Banana in Phyllo Dough

Why is it that chefs never really give much detail in their desserts? On the Starfish menu, this reads: "Fresh banana, cinnamon, salted caramel sauce with vanilla ice cream and fresh berries."

How boring is that? Of course ... having inhaled a few of these and recommended this dessert wildly to nearby diners, I'm not sure I can do much better. Suffice to say that I ... and many people within hearing range of my raves ... have become addicts to this thing. Wrapped in layers of flaky Phyllo, the banana is flash fried and, while still hot, ladled in rich vanilla bean ice cream and the crazy sauce.

Best *Shopping*

Laguna Nursery
1370 S. Coast Hwy • Laguna Beach

Editor's Note: If you walked down any street in Laguna Beach, you know we have A LOT of shopping opportunities. In this Shopping section, I've only chosen a few can't-miss places and items – the best of the best, so to speak, to which residents and tourists flock. And a special note – I've chosen to focus on clothing store reviews in my blog only at www.LagunaBeachBest.com

BUBBLES OF LAGUNA

Best Bath Shop
Bubbles of Laguna
445 S. Coast Highway, Laguna Beach, CA 92651
(949) 494-1417

Hours: 10 a.m. – 7 p.m., summers, 9 a.m. – 9 p.m.

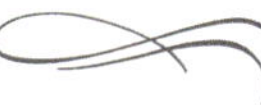

Nestled as a rare storefront in the historical Hotel Laguna in downtown Laguna Beach, Bubbles has been going strong for more than 14 years now.

Its owner, Cathy Wilkinson, offers hundreds of bath items, from every wash, scrub and bead imaginable to nubby shower sponges and "Soapy Soles." The store features its own line of Bubbles shower gels, bath bars and lotions, many of which can be personally scented or mixed to your tastes. And, at least three Laguna Beach residents participate in the store with handmade inventions of their own. It's a cornucopia of gifting for yourself (for starters of course) and any child or adult in your world, and when you've left our lovely town, you have her complete e-commerce store to rely upon.

LAGUNA BEACH BOOKS

1200 S. Coast Highway, Laguna Beach, CA 92651
(949) 494-4779

Hours: 10: a.m. – 8:00 p.m. daily

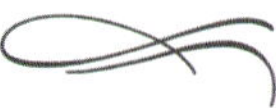

What's a beach without a book? Thanks to Owner Jane Hanauer of Laguna Beach Books in the Old Pottery Place, you have it made in the shade. Here's your haven for popular titles and an additional raft of great books you might never have considered.

This independent bookstore lives up to its name with some of the most eclectic titles in every category you can imagine. Further, the store stocks several racks of the kind of greeting cards you'd like to receive, and you will find a rare collection of art- and photo-centric coffee table books that honor the art-based spirit of our Laguna Beach.

If you're looking for a particular title or author, don't expect to come across a Help Desk with a blank-faced teen. Quite the contrary. Every staff member at Laguna Beach Books (known as "LBB" to locals) not only knows the store's contents inside out and backwards but READS it all, too. These people are some of the most interesting conversationalists you'll find in the entire town of Laguna, and they're extremely helpful in steering you to a memorable read.

The city's recent award recipient as the Laguna Beach Store of the Year, you'll know why the moment you step in this little indy that could.

Insider Tips:

Staff recommendations: The sticky note tags you see throughout the store on all the shelves? These are handwritten recommendations from the staffers on hundreds of books. As I said, these people actually read these books.

Live author events and book signings occur almost weekly. Be sure to sign up at LagunaBeachBooks.com to receive updates on their incoming featured authors. These are regular calendar features that are consistently filled with truly interesting authors.

L.A.-based libraries, foundations and 5-star hotel event managers have come to rely on Laguna Beach Books to provide a specific author's book at their larger speaking events and forums. The LBB folks tote all the credit card machinery, cash banks, books, and knowledgeable staff members along. I've seen them in action – very sophisticated and polished. Check with Owner Jane Hanauer or Manager Lisa Childers for more details.

LAGUNA NURSERY

1370 S. Coast Highway, Laguna Beach, CA 92651
(949) 494-5200

Hours: Mon – Fri 8 a.m. – 5 p.m.; Sat 8 a.m. – 6:00 p.m.;
Sun 9 a.m. – 5:00 p.m.

OK, I know, I know. When you think "Garden Nursery," you think plants, potting soil, maybe a hummingbird feeder or two. And, when Ruben Flores first took over the old nursery space that had,

for the most part, acted the part of a traditional nursery, we figured he was up to the same plan.

But then, none of us had really met Ruben Flores yet.

Ruben is one very cool cat. A landscape architect by degree, Ruben is flown to all parts of the world to work his magic in both individual homes and monstrous public gardens. He is ever and always coming up with new events and parties to host, leads garden Walking Tours on a regular basis and sits on about 17 different boards in the city, including

the Laguna Beach Beautification Committee. (Thanks to him, he and his committee rescued downtown trees that had been consigned to the axe a few months ago.)

He also is the most efficient person I think I've ever met. When Ruben first took over the space for Laguna Nursery, he had that place up and running in a matter of weeks. Now, if you're still thinking "plants, potting soil," sure – not a problem, anyone can get that kind of thing rolling fairly quickly. But Laguna Nursery is way, way beyond that kind of nursery.

You can spend three hours in this place and still not see everything. Laguna Nursery is a veritable wunderkind of magnificence, with room after room done in different themes (from plants to thousands of décor items and live, chatty birds). Outside, it's a jungle of greenery that wraps and wends its way between phenomenal water features and statues.

No matter who's visiting me, Laguna Nursery is a must stop on my list. Ruben has made an art form of the traditional nursery – you simply have to see it to believe it. It's a perfect zen place in the middle of our bustling town.

LAGUNA COLONY

384 Forest Ave., #2, Laguna Beach, CA 92651
(949) 497-8919

Hours: 10:00 a.m. – 6:00 p.m. daily

Where do Laguna Beach locals go for home décor?

While tourists crowd the first block of retail stores on Forest Avenue in Laguna Beach, locals slip right past them, heading just one block further on Forest to their favorite décor and gift store in town, The Colony.

Nestled next to the town's post office since 1994, The Laguna Colony Company is housed in the building that used to be the original lumber yard shop – Laguna Lumber – and is one of the oldest buildings in town. In fact, Laguna Colony's shop's floors are original, dating back to 1913.

Owned by the talented Paul Mosley, Laguna Colony is a treasure trove of one-of-a-kind collections and the hottest trends in jewelry and home fragrances. Paul is a friendly, warm, one-of-a-kind personality and his stores reflect the same - you won't find these pieces anywhere else in Laguna Beach. It's why locals, celebrities and returning travelers from all over the world stop in regularly to see what Paul is featuring this time around. He keeps it fresh, eclectic and very reasonably priced.

While the shop is cozy, you'll want to make a few circles. There are so many great items tucked here and there that you just can't see it all in a single pass. (And if you agree that Laguna Colony rocks during the year, you have to see its transformation during the holiday season. You'll want to buy it all and take it home.)

As just a sampling, The Laguna Colony features:

- Vietri and Mariposa dish and serving ware;
- Aquiesse and Voluspa candles and home fragrances;
- Jellycat stuffed animals in the children's section;
- The latest rage in jewelry – Kim Herbert's line of Charlotte Singleton Silver;
- The Energy Muse Jewelry line, made famous by hundreds of celebrity devotees such as Heidi Klum, Seal, Hillary Duff, David Beckham, Usher, Ryan Seacrest … even Patti LaBelle and former L.A. Lakers Coach Phil Jackson.
- The finest lines of stationery and gift cards.

Your home will thank you, your jewelry box will thank you, and your pet sitters back home will be so pleased that you opted for a sophisticated gift instead of that run-of-the-mill tourist t-shirt.

Given that we have more than 700 registered artists in the city of Laguna Beach, I know my taste in art may not necessarily be that of the general populace. I do know, though, that these three gentlemen are perennial favorites in the Sawdust Festival and they have nothing to do with painting (which makes up a very large portion of our artist population and is, sadly, not my forté). Each also has a studio here in town for year-round shopping.

Best Original Art

John Barber Glassware

Studio & Showroom: 21062 Laguna Canyon Rd,
Laguna Beach, CA 92651
(949) 494-1464

In the late 1960s and early 1970s, John Barber was already making exquisite glassware. He traveled to Germany on invitation to apprentice with the great Erwin Eisch and returned to L.A. three years later to open his own art glass studio. He migrated south a couple years later to live in Laguna Beach, and opened his own studio here a year later.

Sales have always been brisk for John's Art Nouveau glasswork, but when he began demonstrating the art of glass blowing at the Sawdust Festival in the late 1980s, his popularity rocketed. From his intricate barware and wine glasses to immense glass chandeliers and commissioned sculptures, John has a unique style appreciated by celebrities, royalty and plain folk alike.

Mike Brennan Raku Pottery

2225 Laguna Canyon Rd, Laguna Beach, CA 92651
mkbrennan@cox.net

At 16 years of age, Laguna Beach resident Mike Brennan was the youngest artist to be invited to the Sawdust Festival after festival organizers saw the high school sophomore reinstituting the 15th century ceramic art form of Japan – Raku. He continued to participate in the Festival during summer breaks from college and, again, during his tenure at the Art Institute of Southern California. Now, 30-plus years later, he's still throwing his one-of-a-kind Raku pottery and shipping it to every point of the globe (including to a few dear friends of my own!).

Because of his longtime tenure and crowd popularity, you will normally find Mike's booth front-and-center at the Sawdust Festival grounds. He sells – literally – hundreds of pieces during the Sawdust and Winter Fantasy Festivals, which requires untold hours of work as he alone throws each piece and formulates his own glazes. He also participates in numerous commissioned projects, including Wolfgang Puck's upscale restaurants and the Palms Casino Resort in Las Vegas.

Kirk Milette Jewelry

830 S. Coast Highway, Laguna Beach, CA 92651
(949) 497-4653

A couple Sawdust seasons ago, my buddy, Kaj, surprised his girlfriend, Mary, at the Locals Preview Party by stopping at Kirk's booth and asking Kirk (his lifelong buddy) to hand over the custom-made engagement ring he had ordered. Kaj then dropped to one knee to propose to Mary on the sawdust floor.

It was the first time I had met Kirk and really paid attention to his awesome jewelry work, and I've been a devout fan ever since. Kirk attributes his love of art and natural pearls and gems to growing up as a third generation Californian, always "out in the great outdoors."

When he moved to Laguna Beach in the 1960s, Kirk stumbled into jewelry making by first taking a class in the subject as a sophomore. As his initial pieces began winning awards, area jewelers mentored Kirk along as he began to explore the lost art of wax casting.

In 1976, Kirk officially began his custom jewelry business and, a few years later, was invited to participate in the Sawdust Festival. Now, after 30 years at the Sawdust, Kirk's jewelry displays only grow richer in style. He prefers working in exotic pearls, diamonds, sapphires, moonstone and emeralds, but happily designs to unique requests. He has become the "go to" wedding and engagement ring designer for a multitude of Laguna Beach residents, and continues to craft pendants, bracelets, earrings and more.

LAGUNA DRUG

239 Broadway St., Laguna Beach, CA 92651
(949) 715-9206

Hours: 10:00 a.m. – 5:00 p.m. daily

Most of the residents in Laguna Beach probably think of Laguna Drug on Broadway as more of a caterer to our visitors. The enormous store houses plenty of innovative house and kitchen décor, a lot of which boasts the Laguna Beach moniker. At least one-third of the store is devoted to rows of every vitamin, bandage and remedy medicine you could want or need, and even boasts a full-time pharmacy for prescriptions. Its front windows are filled with every beach bag, flip-flop, sunscreen and game supply you could ever want or need for the beach.

It is a constantly busy, constantly thriving store. But don't let the varied sway you from discovering its greatest treasure trove – the greeting card section. While Laguna Colony and Laguna Beach Books do a great job in stocking cards for all reasons and seasons, the selection at Laguna Drug is enormous. In fact, the card section alone takes up at least another third of the Broadway store.

Laguna Drug donates row upon row upon row to its greeting card supply and these are GREAT cards – you know, the kind that actually make you

laugh out loud or get all lumpy-throated. Laguna Drug doesn't seem at all interested in stocking crappy cards. It showcases a large number of vendors, too, including Hallmark, Papyrus, Salty Dog, Design Design and a host of others. Even a couple local artists who've broken into the card business are featured prominently.

At holidays, make this your first stop as well. Valentines abound at the first of the year, only followed with substantial racks dedicated to Easter, Mother's Day, Graduation and even Halloween. At the Christmas and Hanukkah holidays, it's a veritable takeover with hundreds of single card options and stacks and stacks of boxed holiday cards, suitable for every demeanor and fireplace mantel.

Further, you always have boxed invitations, thank you cards, and ready-and-willing clerks who will help you with special and custom orders.

Buzz in for that one card you need, or take a few minutes to peruse and purchase several to stow away for any future occasion. You'll also find a great assortment of boxed cards and stationery any time of the year, and towering edifices of the same during the specific holidays.

MADISON SQUARE & GARDEN CAFÉ

320 N. Coast Highway, Laguna Beach, CA 92651
(949) 494-0137
Hours: Closed Mondays, open daily otherwise,
8:00 a.m. – 3:00 p.m.

We love Madison's proprietor Jon Madison because he doesn't take himself too seriously. Oh yes, the man has serious taste — you can see it from stem to stern in his eclectic Madison Square & Garden Cafe in Laguna Beach, but he has a great sense of humor, too.

The man believes in adding color, magic and fun to your life, especially when it comes to your yard and garden. Heck, even if you have a 6-inch potted plant representing all the greenery in your home, Jon will have something to make that potted plant feel quite queenly.

Aside from the vast number of fountains, wind chimes, Buddha statues and lawn ornaments, Jon's store inside hosts a cornucopia of ingenious home décor items, too. Between outside and in, the offerings are profuse. My advice? Order up a cappuccino at his tiny kitchen and give yourself time to peruse as you wander and sip.

TOOTSIE'S

1200 S. Coast Highway, Laguna Beach, CA 92651
(949) 715-5151

Hours: Mondays 10:00 a.m. – 6:00 p.m.;
Wed – Sat 10:00 a.m. – 7:00 p.m.; Sun 11:00 a.m. – 6:00 p.m.

Nini Drake first opened Tootsie's on Sept. 1st in 2006. Hers was the first to open its doors in the newly revamped Pottery Shack building, and business has been brisk ever since.

The store serves up everything from practical pumps to flirty sandals and trendy autumn and winter boots. Most are designer names, but you're not going to see anything close to the designer pricing you see in the mall stores. Additionally, Nini drives to Los Angeles almost weekly to purchase new bundles of all-season scarves, so the options are always changing out and changing up. They're fabulous finds at ridiculously low prices.

Given that Nini sells women's designer shoes at rock-bottom prices in the first place, her loyal followers red-letter certain calendar days and cancel all other obligations in October and March in expectation of Nini's bi-annual shoe sales. These sales aren't those picked-over, worn-out lookin' kinds of sales. You'll find all sorts of treasures at 50% (and more) off her already low prices. I do my best to advertise these events well in advance at LagunaBeachBest.com/Calendar, but in case you miss the blog announcements, just look for the mob of women outside the front doors.

SUNGLASS GALLERY

205 Ocean Ave., Laguna Beach, CA 92651
(949) 494-5452

Hours: Daily, 10:00 a.m. – 6:00 p.m.

Sunglass Gallery Owner Harry Bagga set up shop nearly 30 years ago, and he's only expanded his presence since. The Gallery houses more than 4,000 sunglasses of every possible designer brand – Oliver Peoples, Louis Vuitton, Tom Ford, Maui Jim, Oakley, Fendi, Ray-Ban, Prada, TAG Heuer, just to name a few. And, Bagga recently expanded again to create a large L-shaped store with entry doors on two different streets – one entry sits on Ocean Avenue (the original entry) while the other sits on PCH directly across from Main Beach.

My best friend, Lisa, turned me onto the Sunglass Gallery about 10 years ago, and I've never gone anywhere since. The service is impeccable and never pushy. The main guys running the store have always been running the store, and they know most of us locals by name. I've broken or needed to repair my Fendis at least 4 times – never a problem and usually fixed in minutes without charge. And, any purchase I make there is on a locals' discount.

These aren't "new rules" that Harry set up to compete with like-minded sunglass companies – this is how it's always been done at Laguna's Sunglass Gallery. Perhaps that's why, after more than two decades, the Sunglass Gallery not only survives every economy, but positively thrives.

LAGUNA SURF & SPORT

1088 S. Coast Highway, Laguna Beach, CA 92651
(949) 497-7000

Hours: 9:00 a.m. – 9:00 p.m. daily

There are a number of good and great surf shops in this town of ours, but none can top the longevity or classic amiability of Laguna Surf & Sport.

This prize corner spot at PCH and Oak Street in South Central Laguna Beach has only and always been a surf shop. Initially the Oak Street Surf Shop in the early 1960s, it proved a perfect "phoenix from the ashes" sort of story when Surf & Sport Founder Eric John moved down from Huntington to open his first surf shop.

Laguna Surf and Sport opened in 1982, and I seriously doubt it's had a dull day since. This place has a surfer vibe from toe to tail, and it's a constant milling ground and community watering hole for homegrown and visiting big names of the sport, including Jeff Booth, Pat O'Conell, Hans Hagen and more. It even had the great luck (ha) of employing Stephen Colletti, the heart throb high schooler of the reality show, *Laguna Beach: The Real Orange County*. Even though the show aired after Stephen had moved on to college, the weekly show spawned thousands of curious visitors and cars stopping to a dead halt on PCH so that teens could sprint across traffic to have their photo taken in front of the store.

As always, Laguna Surf & Sport was – and is – ready for anyone to walk in the door. It's stuffed to the rafters with the latest clothing, gear and boards for surf, snowboard and skate devotees. It doesn't matter whether you're a newbie beginner or an agro advanced pro – Laguna Surf & Sport has it all, or can put its hands on what you need in a matter of hours.

Even better, the enthusiasts behind the counter can field any question you can think to lob at them. One of the first employees under Eric's tutelage, Jason Watson (now the Manager), is the epitome of friendly and he infuses each and every one of his employees with the same.

These folks are running catalogs on every sunglass, skate wheel and beach umbrella circumference in the store. Even more impressive, they're born and bred meteorologists, climatologists and physicists on water temps, incoming swells, hurricane tracking and surf predictions (and direction) in a 20-mile radius. Heck, at one point, when I was desperate to track down the artist to a song I'd found on a kitesurf video, I took my laptop into Laguna Surf & Sport, hoisted it on the counter and had the team listen in – they knew the artist and the song in seven notes.

The store also offers private surf lessons through Jason, and serves as the hub for Steven Chew's ("Sli Dawg") famed summer surf camp (see *Places*). "Basically," says Eric, "We do whatever it takes to introduce anyone and everyone to the great heritage and community of surfing … because once you're a part of it, you know there's nothing else like it in the world."

SOUND SPECTRUM

1264 S. Coast Highway, Laguna Beach, CA 92651
(949) 494-5959

Recently, I took a load of old record albums ... you know, the ones we used to play on turntables ... down to Sound Spectrum, our resident record and CD store in the HIP District of Laguna Beach.

Little did Owner Jim Otto know when he opened in 1967 that he would still be the core of "hipness" in the District itself after all these many years. And, little did he know that "vinyl" music would stop being created in favor of the CD, and that it would come full circle again to re-create a thriving business.

As a "new" record store in 1967 that then became the "used" record store in the 1990s, that's now become "new and used vinyls," Otto says he couldn't have hoped for better. From floor to ceiling, the place is packed with record albums (and some CDs). A tiny back nook proffers tie-dye clothing and actual turntables that are either refurbished or new. Thankfully, the rage for "vinyl" has become such a trend that Otto enjoys a happy side business fixing and selling turntables, too.

When I showed up at his recommended time ("The place will be quieter then," he

said confidently), the place had 6 or 7 people rummaging through albums and pulling this or that album out with a related story to tell his or her tag-along buddy. Each of the mostly-20s-something crowd traded enthusiastic tidbits with Otto, too, who's probably heard it all and still acts surprised.

As I watched Otto quickly flip through my many albums and select 30 or so from the stack, I figured this guy has probably seen it all, too – he knows the sure sales and the rare finds without even consulting a catalog. Given that he's been at this trade for 46 years, he's probably the one who wrote the catalog in the first place.

While it was happy nostalgia for me as I remembered my record store visits of old, it was a treasure trove of newness for most of the visitors I saw there. And, what a great gift-giving idea! Even as I stood there, a young gentleman purchased an armful of vinyls and a turntable for someone's "Sweet 16." Nowadays, many artists' new productions are being created in vinyl format, but imagine introducing the younger generation to the sounds we grew up with.

"The depth and richness on vinyl is just incredible in comparison to what we get in CDs or MP3 versions," says Otto. "Any true music lover is going to love getting back into the world of vinyls."

TIBET HANDICRAFTS

Best Zen Shop

384 Forest Ave., Laguna Beach, CA 92651
(949) 715-1043

Hours: 10:00 a.m. – 5:00 p.m. daily

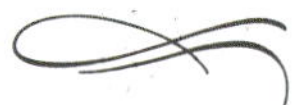

Tenpa Dorjee's Tibet Handicrafts isn't just a unique store – it's a door to an entirely different world.

From his boyhood years in an orphanage in Tibet, Tenpa wanted to create a business that would have meaning and significance. In 1998, after immigrating to the United States, Tenpa decided that his store would support the Tibetan refugees who had been forced to flee their native country. As he began hunting for the perfect store location in Orange County, he jumped feet first into the import of all the items he would sell in his store, tapping into Tibetan arenas in India, Nepal and Thailand.

Over years of research, Tenpa began stockpiling dresses, scarves, prayer flags, jewelry and singing bowls, all the while still looking for the perfect place to set up shop.

It wasn't until 2010, when his Buddhist master was visiting, that Tenpa and his Master wandered into Laguna Beach and the Coffee Pub on Forest Street. As they sat on the patio sipping their drinks, his master noticed that the space next to the coffee shop was up for lease. He turned to Tenpa and said, "This place is meant for you." He then stood and blessed the door, hanging a prayer tassel on a hook just above the address plate of the store.

A week later, Tenpa had his store location. What Tenpa has brought to our community, though, is far more than the beautiful, handmade

items, books, statues and music of the Tibetan culture. Within months of settling in Laguna Beach, Tenpa helped organize a visit of Tibetan monks who, over a week's time, created a beautiful sand mandala at the Congregational Church in Laguna Beach. It was an awe-inspiring event, to say the least (See Sand Mandala story, *Events*). The monks have returned a second time because of the warm reception they received in Laguna, and Tenpa is busy organizing their next visit.

Tenpa also brings in Buddhist masters and speakers for special events, and he's heavily involved in projects that purchase and deliver solar lanterns to families in India. Whenever he gets Laguna Beach residents involved, he's the first to cook up massive "thank you dinners" in reciprocation. Small wonder that Tenpa's store thrives as he is finally fulfilling his boyhood dream – a business that provides so much meaning and significance.

Best
Weekly
&
Monthly
Events

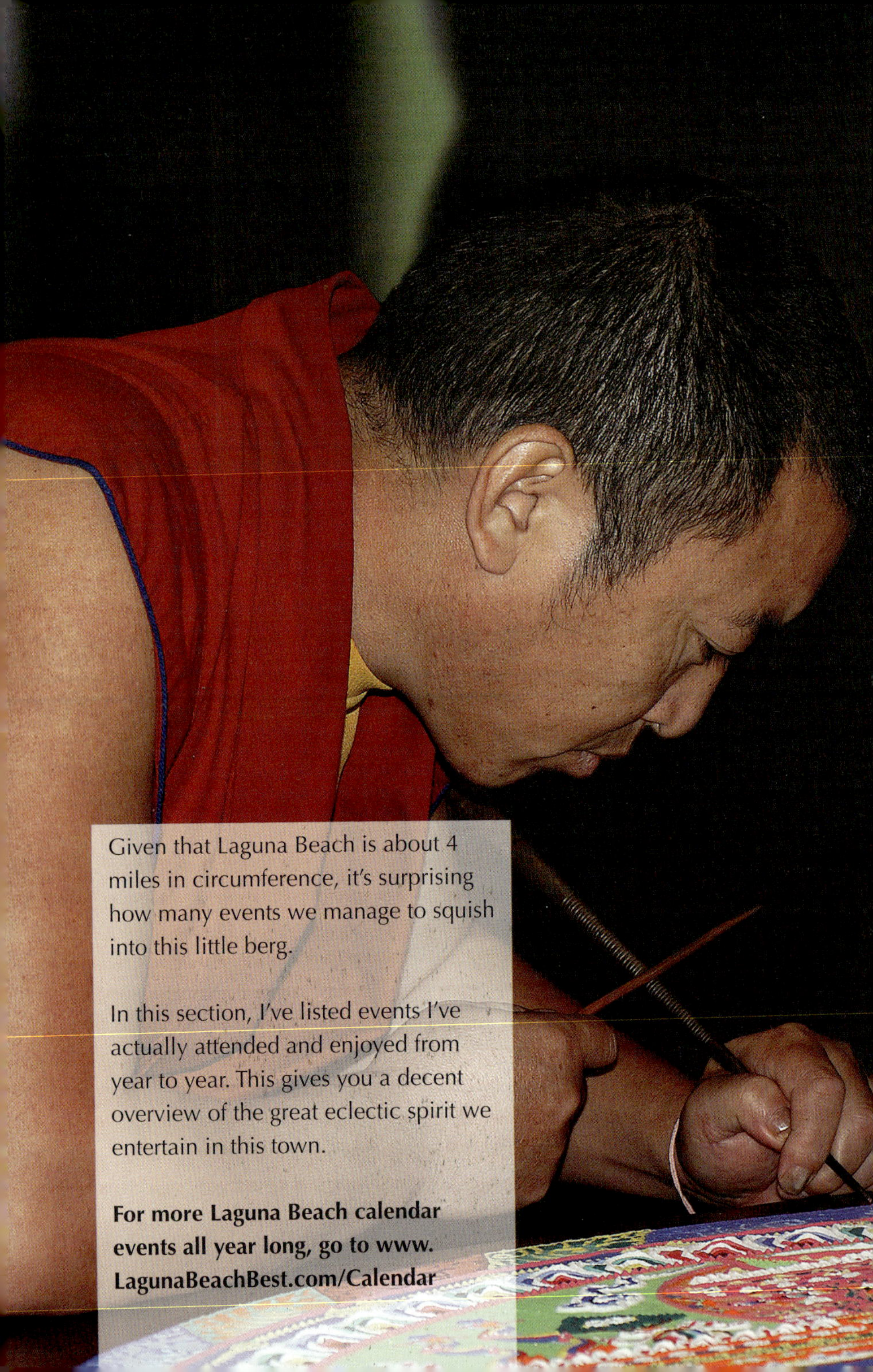

Given that Laguna Beach is about 4 miles in circumference, it's surprising how many events we manage to squish into this little berg.

In this section, I've listed events I've actually attended and enjoyed from year to year. This gives you a decent overview of the great eclectic spirit we entertain in this town.

For more Laguna Beach calendar events all year long, go to www. LagunaBeachBest.com/Calendar

WEEKLY EVENTS

Farmer's Market

Every Saturday next to City Hall
Downtown Laguna Beach
8:00 a.m. – noon
No entry fee

For years now, and on every Saturday morning in Laguna Beach, the Certified Farmer's Market has served Laguna Beach residents and tourists with great produce, flowers, local honey, homemade delicacies and more from at least 40 vendors and farmers. (Don't miss the empanadas!) Because this Farmer's Market is in Laguna Beach, you will also find a very decent arts and crafts fair, too. Hours are from 8:00 to noon in the Lumberyard Parking Lot on Forest Avenue. (Just look for the crossing guards on duty.)

Saturday Morning Live Jazz Jam, Laguna Coffee

1050 S. Coast Highway, Laguna Beach, CA 92651
10:00 a.m. – 12:30 p.m.
Free event (but buying a coffee would be nice on your end)

I've already introduced you to Laguna Coffee Company and its amazing desserts already. While Laguna Coffee is always hopping with activity, great music and chatter, it hops at a whole new level on Saturdays during the Laguna Coffee Saturday Morning Live Jazz Jam.

At about 9:00, you will see local professional musicians wheeling in BIG instruments – we're not talking clarinets here ... we're talking full-on pianos, cellos, electric guitars, and enough horns to fill a symphony.

These guys squish and jam themselves into about 6 square feet of space and proceed to fill every corner of the place with the finest jazz you will hear. People crowd in, shoulder to shoulder, and overflow to the tables and street beyond for a solid two hours as the boys go to town. If you're a jazz fan of ANY age, this is a fun Saturday morning venture any time of the year.

MONTHLY EVENTS

Full Moon Drum Circle

Aliso State Beach, 31131 S. Coast Highway, Laguna Beach CA 92652
sunset – 10:00 p.m.
Free event

Truly one of the more eclectic events in all of Laguna Beach, the monthly Full Moon Drum Circle at Aliso Beach comes compliments of Billy Fried's LaVida Laguna Adventure Company.

Years ago, Billy began a drum circle to celebrate the full moon at Fisherman's Cove off of Heisler Park. It proved so popular on its very first run that he had to relocate the following month to a much bigger beach – Aliso State Beach (or Aliso Creek to us locals).

Starting right at dusk and until the park closes at 10:00 p.m., this is a rare event to behold. Professional and amateur percussion drummers circle around a growing bonfire and just drum to their hearts' content. Sit back and enjoy the rhythm, or stand up and shake your bootie to the beat – nobody minds. On summer weekends, you will also see fire dancers and jugglers participating near the circle, lining Aliso Beach with their flame and shadows.

Bring a drum, blankets, and any food for yourself or your party. (If you don't have a drum, you're still welcome, of course.) Hauling in extra wood for the bonfire sets you out as a hero immediately.

First Thursday of every month

The Laguna Beach ArtWalk

Galleries open throughout North, Main and South Laguna Beach
5:30 p.m. – 10:00 p.m.
Free event

On the first Thursday of every month, Laguna Beach hosts its famous ArtWalk.

Now, as you may or may not know, Laguna Beach was first established as an art colony that soon attracted Hollywood (and the rest of the world) to its scene. But, when you have more than 200 galleries and artist studios in Laguna Beach, ranging from sculpture to oil paintings, it can sometimes be overload to even the most ardent art admirers. The ArtWalk was a great solution to allow art lovers the freedom to peruse a number of galleries beyond normal operating hours.

On ArtWalk nights, Laguna Beach art gallery owners throw open their doors to passing public. Local retailers and coffee shops follow suit. You will find plenty of live artist demonstrations, wine, cocktails, munchies and live music everywhere you go. In many cases, you will meet the artists themselves for a bit of conversation about their work.

Free shuttles operate all the night long between north Laguna galleries, downtown galleries and south/Hip District galleries. For me, I prefer to hoof it with friends as we always manage to happen upon a gallery we missed in the last month's crossing.

Laguna Beach Garden Walking Tours with Laguna Beach's Best Docent

starts at Laguna Nursery
1370 S. Coast Highway, Laguna Beach, CA 92651
10:00 a.m. – noon
Free event

Just about every three weeks, the always-surprising Ruben Flores (owner of Laguna Nursery) is seen shepherding newbie and pro gardeners alike to Laguna Beach's public and private gardens in his 2-hour tours. (Check www.LagunaBeachbest.com/Calendar for specific dates.)

"I started the tours because so many people just zip down the main thoroughfares of Laguna – even the residents themselves get into certain driving patterns – and they never see the amazing landscaping and gardens of so many homes in the quieter, auxiliary streets," says Ruben.

The tours are, for the most part, simple rambles. "I might have specific gardens in mind, but in many cases, we'll just stop and knock at someone's door and ask if we can see their backyard," says Flores. "Much politer than poking our noses over their fences, don't you think?"

But this isn't just a tour for admiring oohs and ahhs. Ruben Flores talks through shade and sun, salt-water proximity issues, herb-lined walking paths, flowering hedges, xeriscaping and irrigating. A globally renowned landscape architect by trade, Ruben knows just about every flower, tree, hedge, herb and garden bug known to this planet.

Now you have the opportunity to pick up some great tips and advice, and learn how to create your own garden with green thumb magic. Grab your coffee, put on a pair of good walking shoes, and head down to Laguna Nursery by 10:00 a.m.

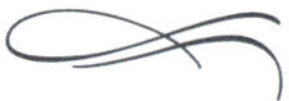

The Laguna Nursery Cabaret

1370 S. Coast Highway, Laguna Beach CA 92651
6:00 p.m. – 10:00 p.m.
Tickets are $40 in advance, $50 at door
Check the LagunaBeachBest.com/Calendar for specific dates.

Laguna Nursery owner Ruben Flores came up with the idea of an "occasional" cabaret evening in his nursery about a year and a half ago, and the idea took off like a rodeo bull. In the "high season" (summer, holidays), Ruben creates a Cabaret Evening just about every single month, and people in this town rave about it.

"When I create gardens for people, I always include speakers because I think music and gardens are supposed to go together," says Ruben. "And,

when you're in our nursery at night with all the lights and greenery around you, the music is just phenomenal."

The giant nursery clears space in the middle, lights its spectacular chandeliers, and hauls in a grand piano to cater to professional piano players and singers from all over the world. Residents and visitors pile in for catered food, beverage, spectacular music and, yes, even sing-alongs.

JANUARY

Third week of January

***Laguna Beach Live!* presents Winter Jazz Series**

[seven-degrees], 891 Laguna Canyon Road, Laguna Beach, CA 92651
Every Wednesday, 5:00 p.m. – 8:30 p.m.
Tickets are $15 per person

There's no better cure for our brisk January temperatures than the toe-tapping, hand-clapping, get-up-and-move jazz concerts that return the third week of January.

Every other Wednesday through mid-April, *Laguna Beach Live!* is brings back the finest regional and national jazz talents in its *Jazz Wednesdays* concert series at the acoustically perfect [seven-degrees] event center. Tickets for each event are just $15 when purchased in advance – www.LagunaBeachLive.org – or $20 at the door (if still available). Even though these are globally renowned musicians on stage, it's this non-profit's mission to introduce great music to anyone and everyone, so they've kept their ticket prices ridiculously low. The *Laguna Beach Live!* summer and winter *Jazz Wednesdays* series has grown so popular that more people are purchasing the entire 7-concert season for just $105 to ensure front-of-house seating.

Whether you pick and choose concerts, or pile in for all seven, you're in for a rare treat. A full bar and menu is also available for additional purchase during each event, so grab your friends and make a night of it.

January (end of January)

Chinese New Year's Week-Long Celebration, Starfish Asian Cuisine

30832 S. Coast Highway, Laguna Beach, CA 92651

5:30 p.m. – close

In keeping with a tradition that runs several thousand years deep, Starfish Asian Cuisine in South Laguna Beach always celebrates the Chinese New Year in style. At least a week long, Starfish creates an exclusive menu along with unpublished drink specials to pay homage to the incoming Chinese New Year critter. Then, as the Chinese wrap up their primary 4-day New Year celebration, Starfish ramps up the party with live music and guest mixologists creating rather stunning, one-of-a-kind drinks. Starfish is in the Haggen's shopping center directly across from the Montage Laguna Beach.

FEBRUARY

Second weekend of February

Laguna Beach Music Festival

Tickets go on sale in September at LagunaBeachMusicFestival.com

Now an annual event, this is an impressive, weeklong event co-presented by *Laguna Beach Live!* and the Philharmonic Society of Orange County.

A number of big-name musicians, bands, quartets and quintets converge on Laguna, presenting concerts in various intimate settings throughout downtown Laguna Beach and at the Laguna Playhouse. It seems that, no matter where you walk this week, you'll find your steps accompanied by music from any number of simultaneous venues.

During the same week, the Music Festival provides insider peeks to rehearsals and meet-the-artist events, along with concerts and fun events at the schools. Purchase package tickets for concerts and hob-nobbing events, or purchase individually as you see fit.

Photo credit: M. Felt Photography

First Saturday of February

Annual Art Auction, Laguna Art Museum

307 Cliff Drive, Laguna Beach, CA 92651

In February at the Laguna Art Museum, the renowned annual Art Auction has its day.

The Art Auction draws more than 400 attendees to bid on original works done by more than 110 artists. It's the Museum's largest fund raiser, and has become a well-known party for all, as the festivities go on for several hours into the evening.

Initially, the art is in place the week prior to the auction for viewing. On that Saturday evening, the bedecked and bejeweled arrive for a large cocktail and appetizers party that normally features more than 10 restaurants and wine and liquor vendors. It's a happy, high-brow evening of cheese and wine pairings, small bites of signature dishes, vintage-inspired cocktails, and more.

Silent auction items are available for bid through the first couple of hours of the event, and then the live (and very lively) live auction begins. It's a great way to learn about emerging artists, bid on new favorites and support the Art Museum, all in a single evening.

MARCH

Laguna Beach Annual Patriot's Day Parade

Starts at Laguna Beach High School, ends at Fire Station on Forest Avenue
11:00 a.m. – 1:00 p.m.
Free event

We're nearly at the 50-year mark for the Laguna Beach Patriot's Day Parade and, at this point, I'm not sure enough of the founding fathers are around to tell us how this ginormous parade was organized in the first place. Fact is, this is the largest parade in Laguna Beach all the year long, and as long as it continues to honor our patriots, we're all happy to participate.

Participation, actually, is huge in the Patriot's Day Parade. It organizes itself at the high school on Park Avenue, and winds its way into downtown Laguna Beach to end in front of the fire station where dignitaries are seated.

This parade honors everybody, from Citizen of the Year to Athlete of the Year and Essay Contest Winner of the Year. The parade line-up rivals the Rose Bowl Parade with more than 100 entries, from restaurants to bookstores to gas stations and teachers … even the Laguna Laughter Club participates

photo credit: Mary Hurlbut, MaryHurlbutPhoto.com

(and happily!). If you're someone who loves Laguna Beach, man, you're in the parade.

Streets lock down. Traffic is blocked for miles. Streets are lined several people deep with flag-waving adults and kids. It is – dare I say? – larger than the Santa Claus Parade on our annual Hospitality Night.

Oddly, the neighboring city of Dana Point chooses the very same day every year to do its enormous Annual Festival of the Whales Parade, so if you're in a car trying to get somewhere in this 10-mile stretch of PCH, just forget about it. Park, pay an extreme amount for parking, and resolve to enjoy your day watching a parade.

EASTER

This a quick look at Laguna Beach Easter Egg hunts, Easter Egg coloring events and Easter brunches on Easter Sunday. While these events have been going on for a very long time, please check LagunaBeachBest.com for updates (I'd hate to see you at an empty, grassy knoll with no Easter Bunny treats to be found.)

On Easter Sunday:

Annual Laguna Beach Easter Egg Hunt

1:00 p.m., Laguna Beach High School, 625 Park Avenue,
Laguna Beach, CA 92651

For more than 50 years, the American Legion has been finding a way to produce THE Easter Bunny for all the Laguna Beach kids. (No kidding! These people have serious connections.) Come on down at 1:00 Easter Sunday for this can't miss Easter Egg Hunt. Kids 9 years of age and younger are invited to bring empty Easter baskets and participate in the free activities. Arrive early for pictures with the Easter Bunny.

On Easter:

Annual Laguna Beach Easter Egg Coloring Event

9 a.m. – 1 p.m., Madison Square Garden & Cafe,
320 N. Coast Highway, Laguna Beach, CA 92651

Owner Jon Madison is at it again with Laguna Beach's most famous Easter Egg Coloring Event. This year, he's planning to boil up about 200-300 eggs, and provides all the stencils, colors, and dipping sauce any kid might need for that masterpiece egg. As Madison's is one of the dog-friendliest places in town, you're welcome to pack up kids and dogs and head on down for some great (if a little chaotic) fun. (You might have to help your dogs with the Easter egg dipping ... it's that whole opposable thumb issue, poor things.)

For a complete Easter Brunch and Dining Directory go to www. LagunaBeachBest.com

APRIL

Spring Fling Festival, South Laguna Community Garden

Eagle Rock Way between PCH and Virginia
2:00 p.m. – 5:00 p.m.
Free event

Perched at Eagle Rock Way and PCH on what used to be scrubby vacant lot dirt, the South Laguna Community Garden is now a mecca of privately owned garden plots, kids' gardens, picnic tables and hand-chiseled benches. No matter what the time of day, you will find any number of people tilling the soil, harvesting their own "crops," or sipping coffee with a friend on one of the handy benches.

Mind you, it was no small feat to put this Community Garden in place. While my good friend, Morrie Granger, was the first to get the idea rolling back in 2009, there were lines of people willing to "rent" a garden box of their own (there's still a waiting list today). And, there were many gracious donors to this little neighborhood project, including the South Coast Water District, many businesses and individuals and Ruben Flores' Laguna Nursery's massive help with dirt, boxes and free gardening workshops.

Community Garden's Soil is Now Sold

Now that the Community Garden stretches to every corner of the vacant lot, the owner who originally agreed to the land being cleared and tilled has sold the property. The folks behind the garden are working diligently with the city, Laguna businesses and private donors to find new digs and the new owner is taking his time with new plans.

For the time being, the South Laguna Community Garden continues to celebrate its happy existence by asking anyone and everyone to join them at their FREE Spring Fling Festival and Potluck every April. Bring a potluck dish to share, pack in your own drinks, and participate in live entertainment, children's activities, cooking demonstrations, and more. It's a great, annual neighborhood event that has quickly gathered and collected surrounding neighborhoods and communities to its leafy, green bosom.

"Green Eggs and AM" Amateur Skimboard Contest

South Laguna Beach location (usually Aliso Beach or West Street Beach)
7:30 a.m. – 4:00 p.m.
For participants:
$20 entry fee,
$10 final stage fee

This event is a genius brainchild on the parts of Exile Skimboard's SteveTaylor and Paulo Prietto, both longtime

Side note here: At each year's event thusfar several international skimboard pros take to the water for a surprise heat of their own. Last time I watched, the great Sammie Stinnett walked with the Green Eggs Pro Crown. So, you never know what the pros might decide to do as they support the up-and-comers.

pro skimboarders in the international circuit. Why not start getting an eye on the up-and-coming groms (and older guys, too) in the skimboarding haven of Laguna Beach?

Aptly titled Green Eggs and AM, the amateur skimboard divisions are categorized by ability, not age. Loraxes are beginners; Sneetches are the Intermediates; and Grinches are the Advanced boarders. Taylor says most amateurs self-qualify, but they're happy to help anyone who's not sure which Seuss category he/she belongs.

Clipboards open around 8:00ish, with the event beginning around 9:00-9:30. Check out updates and details at: facebook.com/GreenEggsandAm

MAY

Heisler Park Sunset Serenades

Friday evenings in May
Free event

Much like the gorgeous grounds at the Montage Resort, Laguna Beach's Heisler Park is an immaculate, beautiful expanse that rolls just north of Main Beach, up and along Cliff Drive. Because of its closer proximity to downtown Laguna Beach, Heisler certainly gets more foot traffic than the Montage, but you sure couldn't guess, given the care and maintenance it receives.

The Heisler Park "amphitheater" is more of a small stone stage with tiered seating areas and a sweeping, grassy slope above. It offers extremely great views of the ocean and is always a hub for creative art at its best.

In May, the free Sunset Serenades are an annual rite welcoming summer. Pack up your beach chairs or beach blankets, and load up a basket of favorites munchies and a covert bottle of wine for great evenings of live jazz, acoustic rock, folk and country. It's definitely a locals' hob-nobbing kind of event, and a hoot all around for all ages.

Main Beach Women's AAA Volleyball Open

8:30 a.m. – 4:00 p.m.

Sanctioned by the City and CBVA, watch as top-ranked players and local stand-outs battle it out on the sand in what is becoming one of the largest participation events in Southern California. The women's event draws quite a crowd – be sure to bring your beach chairs, towels and plenty of sunscreen. (See the Men's Volleyball Event in June's calendar.)

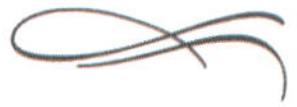

MOTHER'S DAY

See the complete Mother's Day Dining Directory for Laguna Beach at www.LagunaBeachBest.com

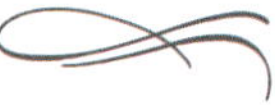

Third Sunday of May

Charm House Tour

12:00 p.m. – 5:00 p.m.

$45 per person, tour shuttles included

Each year, and always on the Sunday after Mother's Day, the Village Laguna folks roll out an impressive tour of five homes. One of

Laguna's finest features lies in the fact that no two houses are the same in this eclectic berg, and the Charm House Tour in Laguna Beach makes this quite evident. For many years, hundreds have flocked to the Tour; it makes for a fun afternoon of new architecting and decor ideas.

Normally, the Charm House Tour Shuttles load passengers at the Festival grounds in Laguna Canyon or in South Laguna at the Mission Hospital (PCH & 7th Avenue) depending on where in town the tour is taking place. (Free parking is allowed for Tour participants at the hospital's parking structure.)

At any time from noon to 5:00 p.m., Tour participants can drop in at their leisure, so no need to bustle out there to be on the busses at noon. The tour itself is about 1.5 – 2 hours in length, so choose a time, take a buddy, and enjoy yourself!

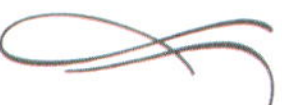

Pacific Marine Mammal Martini Madness

Photo credit: Wendy Saewert

Hosted by Madison Square Garden & Café,
320 N. Coast Highway,
Laguna Beach, CA 92651
5:00 p.m. – 7:00 p.m.

Tickets online at www.pacificmmc.org/events.html

Leave it to Jon Madison, the fun-loving personality behind Madison Square Garden & Café, to produce a fantastic event on behalf of downtrodden seals.

Each year, on the Sunday after Mother's Day, in his efforts to help the only marine mammal rehabilitation center in Orange County (right here in Laguna Beach), Jon sponsors a fantastic party – Martini Madness. This fast-growing event is one of Laguna's most popular fun evenings as attendees are treated to live music and delectable martini creations from guest host bartenders.

It's all done in the name of our dear, sick seals and sea lions, an appalling number of which have been finding their way to our beaches and rocky shores lately. This year, our early months saw an unbelievable number of patients waddling their way on shore, and the Pacific Marine Mammal Center has been overrun with hundreds of patients who are sick, dehydrated and wounded.

While marine biologists up and down the coast are trying to sort the reason for this vast exodus from the seas, the PMMC's hospital operation in Laguna Canyon continues to take in as many as it can possibly handle, relying solely on public support and donations to help these lovely critters rest and recover. (The PMMC is a non-profit organization and 95% volunteer run by staffers and veterinarians.)

The Martini Madness party is a great way to bring so many Laguna Beach locals and visitors together for this cause. With tickets so inexpensive, I would hope the entire lot of you readers out there will purchase a ticket, even if you live in Anchorage, Alaska. The seals and sea lions thank you.

Memorial Day Pancake Breakfast
Heisler Park, Myrtle Street and Cliff Drive
7:00 a.m. – 10:30 a.m.

At Memorial Day and Labor Day, you can always count on one thing to remain constant: pancake flipping by Laguna's finest. For years now (probably decades), the Laguna Exchange Club teams with Laguna Beach Police and Firefighters host a $5 flapjack breakfast. Locals line up by the hundreds, and tourists lucky enough to stumble across the event join right in, too.

The Pancake Breakfast is a major fundraiser for the Exchange Club, with all its proceeds donated to child abuse prevention and community youth projects.

Life in Laguna Beach

Chef Amar of Broadway Restaurant dishes up another monthly wine dinner.

JUNE

Main Beach Men's AAA Volleyball Open

8:30 a.m. – 4:00 p.m.

Sanctioned by the City and CBVA, watch as top-ranked players and Laguna Beach local stand-outs battle it out on the sand in what is becoming one of the largest participation events in Southern California. The men's event draws quite a surprising number of well-known pros, and the onlookers and fans are always in for an exciting show. Be sure to bring your beach chairs, towels and plenty of sunscreen. (See the Women's Event in May's calendar.)

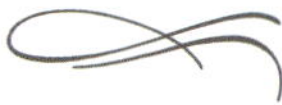

Mid-June through end of August

Jazz Wednesdays at The Ranch

31106 S. Coast Highway, Laguna Beach, CA 92651
Tickets at www.LagunaBeachLive.org

This is such a popular event that the weekly jazz sessions are normally sold out several weeks in advance. Jazz Wednesdays is the brainchild of the ever-innovative *Laguna Beach Live!* organization, a non-profit devoted to introducing all sorts of live music to Laguna Beach without the large price tag.

They sure hit their mark with this one. The annual event takes place every other Wednesday for just a few short weeks on the open-air patio at the beautiful Ranch for the 2-hour concert. Concerts bring in some

photo credit: LagunaBeachLive.org

of the finest professional jazz talent on global dockets, and tickets are ridiculously low priced. It's a beautiful outdoor concert venue with plenty of great food and drink available for purchase to make an evening of it.

End of June through August

Summer Camp Pinniped – The Pacific Marine Mammal Center Day Camp

(7 week-long camps)

(see full details, *Places Locals Go*)

End of June through August

Laguna Beach's (Famous) Summer Surf School by Sli Dawg

(10 camps offered)

(see full details, *Places Locals Go*)

End of June through 1st of September

The Sawdust Arts & Crafts Festival

935 Laguna Canyon Road, Laguna Beach, CA 92651
10 a.m. – 10 p.m. daily (closes at 6:00 p.m. on July 4th)
Wheelchair accessible. Service animals only allowed on the grounds.

Avoid long lines, purchase day and season tickets online:
http://www.sawdustartfestival.org/tickets
All military and family admitted FREE with military ID

If you're in Laguna Beach for just a DAY between the end of June and the first day of September, this is an event you've got to see. Begun by a rogue element of Laguna Beach resident artists decades ago, the Sawdust has grown up to house more than 200 artists from every make and model of art media you can imagine.

Laguna Beach's Sawdust Art Festival is every type and kind of art imaginable – jewelry, ceramics, glass sculpture, photography of every possible thing you can photograph, Raku pottery, oil paintings, acrylics paintings, watercolors, watercolor tie dye on fabric, fabric purses, wire art, pen-and-ink drawing, brass sculpture, wood carvings and ... when they can't figure what else to call it ... "mixed media" is in the bag, too.

Folks like Michael Ezzel, Walter Reiss, John Eagle and Kirk Milette have practically been here since the Sawdust began (imagine 30+ years of day-in and day-out booth sitting at Laguna's Sawdust Festival. That's commitment!). Others, like booth mates Dedre Bickler-Sines and Paulette Auster have just passed single and double-digit years at the Festival. Raku favorite Mike Brennan is still on record for being the youngest artist ever invited to the Sawdust nearly two decades ago, while another young artist I met – Art "Z" – received his first invitation this year.

I think what I love most about the Sawdust is getting to know such a wide variety of personalities and "back stories" in these amazing artists. They're live and in color, and what a bunch of great colors you'll see coming at you. At the same time, you actually have decent food and drink here at the Sawdust; live music; all sorts of kids' workshops; and additional art classes you can participate in throughout the Sawdust season.

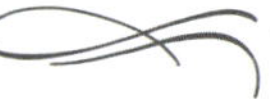

Mid-June, Saturday and Sunday

Victoria Skimboard World Championships

South Laguna Beach location (usually Aliso Beach or West Street Beach)
7:30 a.m. – 4:00 p.m.
Registration online: http://thevic.victoriaskimboards.com/registration/

This is the Grandpappy skimboarding event of all skimboarding events – The Victoria Skimboards World Championship of Skimboarding (aka, "The Vic.") Grab your friends and a couple of beach blankets and park yourself at this phenomenal event. (Oh, and don't forget the sunscreen. We all got crispified like bacon last year.)

Laguna Beach is where skimboarding was born. For 30 years, Tex Haines and the Prietto family, co-founders of Victoria Skimboards, have endeavored to make the sport of skimboarding a worldwide event. The great thing about the skimboard culture is the personality and warmth – these guys are not arrogant by any stretch. They don't take themselves

too seriously. These skimboarders still talk with the common folk, and offer suggestions to groms and oldies alike. This culture is largely due to what Haines and Prietto insisted upon in the early days, and it's almost reverential to see their influence in every aspect of the sport in every corner of the world.

For nine years now, I've been photographing the amateur and pro skimboarders at this event – (I have photos of Blair Conklin back when he was just a tiny grom looking on.) After traveling around after these guys in their various contest locations, I can safely say that "The Vic" is THE place to see the most pro skimboarders gathered from all parts of the world.

"The Vic" sits midstride in the season's United Skim Tour. More than 100 professional skimboarders from all over the world compete in this event, and the amateur classes just keep getting larger in number (last year, the 15-17 year old category almost outranked the number of pros competing). The Vic has a way of upending year-to-date standings, clearly separating the top of the pro charts from the contenders in Aliso Beach's take-no-prisoners waters.

Further, given that most of the top 10 skimboarders in the entire world were raised in South Laguna Beach, you know the best skimboarders are always having a party on their own home turf … and this is a party you want to see.

There's no better place to see the best talent in the skimboarding world, and no better place to see emerging talent make its way from grom amateur status to pro potential. Everything starts rolling around 7:30 on Saturday morning. The pros usually start their first heats a couple hours thereafter, but that ETA is always a moving target, based on what Tex Haines sees the ocean doing out there. All age classes compete to semi-final status, and the games begin again, bright and early on Sunday, through the final heats and the crowning of the new reigning champion.

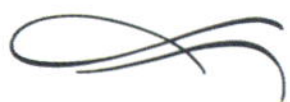

End of June through August

Pageant of the Masters

Festival Art Show & Free Docent Tours

Pageant of the Masters Grounds
650 Laguna Canyon Road, Laguna Beach, CA 92651
June 30 – July 4: 10:00 a.m. – 6:00 p.m. daily
July 5 – Aug. 31: 10 a.m. – 11:30 p.m. daily
Aug. 24: 10 a.m. – 3:30 p.m.
Wheelchair accessible. Service animals only are allowed on the grounds.

Purchase day and season passes online at www.foapom.com
All military and family admitted FREE with military ID
Laguna Beach locals: FREE with ID

In conjunction with Laguna Beach's world-renowned Pageant of the Masters, the Pageant's Festival of Arts Art Show is a rich exhibit of local and national artists, which includes demonstrations, art workshops, daily art tours, live music and more.

For me, it all came together when I discovered that the Festival of Arts offers FREE Docent Tours of all the artwork, Monday through Friday at 11:00 a.m., and on every weekday but Monday, again from 3:00 – 4:00 p.m. On Saturday, there's one art tour at 4:00 p.m.

What a great idea and what a great way to see the Festival of Arts! So, I gathered up a posse of friends and we all headed down for our free tour.

We met up with a lovely lady, Sydelle, at the Information Booth, and she was off and trotting in seconds with her brood waddling behind her. In one short hour, she showed us around to about 75% of the booths, offering tidbit stories; information on medium and original artist style; and all sorts of interesting facts and factoids about the artists that you'd rarely learn, even in talking to the artist personally.

Seriously, where else could you possibly learn that ...

- Raymond Caruso, the scrimshaw artist, only carves from naturally shed walrus tusk
- Jeweler Gretchen Shields eschewed traditional jewel display boxes to house her big, bold jewelry in MUCH more interesting fashion …
- Noriho Uriu is known as the "suicide artist" because …
- Shelley Rapp Evans has carried the centuries-old tradition of "Spirit Keepers" into her popular work …
- Rick Graves devised his own camera to preserve the images he finds …
- Ceramic renown Marlo Bartels knew he wanted to be in ceramics while still in high school, so he traced ceramics back to its origination and took off for the Middle East to live there, exploring every facet and factory he could find …

- John Taylor produces his magnificent 3-dimensional ships from tiny pieces of refuse he finds …
- Rose Hammer taught herself how to make exquisite baskets out of nothing but pine needles …

This was a fun, engaging tour at the Festival of Arts. I respect and admire anyone who can bring the story of original artwork to life, and Sydelle did a really fabulous job. No doubt, every volunteer docent at the Festival of Arts does the same.

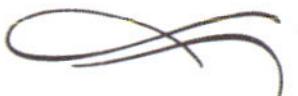

MAYBE JUNE … MAYBE JULY … MAYBE AUGUST

The Oh-So-Secret, Brotherhood-Of-The-Ring Annual Brooks Street Surf Classic

Brooks Street Reef
Date always to be determined. Follow www.facebook.com/BestofLagunaBeach for sudden and urgent updates.

The contest is open to Laguna Beach locals only. Entry fee is $20. Divisions include Girls, Boys, Women, Men, Senior Men, Masters, Senior Masters, Grand Masters, Long Boarders, Body Boarders, Paddle boarders and Pro-Am.

Each year, for 50 years now, the surfers of Laguna Beach send out secret decoder ring anagrams and smoke signals to fellow amateur and pro surfers when the swell is most admirable at Brooks Street. They wait for the opportune time, the opportune swell ... and they might wait for years without sending out the Batman signal.

Lately, though, it seems to have become an annual event … and it's an incredible event. If you're lucky enough to be a friend of a surfer or just some haphazard peep on the beach, you're in for a show.

Surfers of all ages suddenly converge, and we usually see a number of pro surfers on quick sabbatical from the U.S. Surfing Classic up in Huntington Beach, too. Grab your joe (that's "coffee" to you non-Southern Calis) and hoof it down to Brooks Street – there's a small built-in viewing area and hundreds of fans there. Can't miss it.

Ongoing Events

Editor's Note: Many events, festivals and summer camps begun in May and June continue through the months of July and August. Please return to their initial write-ups on the previous pages for information and dates.

INDEPENDENCE DAY

Heisler Park (North of Main Beach)

Every year, we wait with bated breath, wondering if the City is going to follow through on a Laguna Beach 4th of July fireworks show. This happens every year, of course, because rumors always fly that the event will be cancelled (horrors).

But for the purposes of this book, we're going to assume the upcoming 4th of July Fireworks show is ON (I'm not sure how we could keep the marauding hordes out anyway if we tried.) The primary Laguna show originates from Monument Point at Heisler Park. So, here's the official scoop: The Point itself is closed the entire 4th of July day. And, at 5:00 p.m., the area of Heisler Park from Myrtle Street to Rockpile Beach (Jasmine Street) is closed, too. The fireworks show begins at about 9:00 p.m.

City trolleys operate from 9:30 a.m. – 7:00 p.m. and they do NOT resume after the show. Keep this in mind as you will be hoofing it to wherever your car is parked after the 25-minute show has faded from the night sky.

Now, granted, the City does everything it can to help people exit Laguna Beach after the fireworks show, but if I were you, I'd settle into one of the local pubs or fine food establishments and wait it out about an hour. Even though Laguna Canyon Road will open its center lane to allow for two lanes of traffic OUT of town … trust me … hang out, relax and let the mad dust settle.

If you choose to stake your grass or beach claim earlier in the day, keep the following rules in mind:

- No alcohol or smoking on the beaches.
- No tents, canopies or barbeques.
- No dogs are allowed from 9 a.m. to 6 p.m.
- Don't even think about setting off your own fireworks (wherever you might be squatting in the city boundaries) as every sign already posted into Laguna Beach tells you this is an illegal activity. They mean it. It's already a dry season, and the city will have patrols posted everywhere.

Note, too, that Emerald Bay's homeowner's association does its own fireworks show, and it's nothing to sneeze at. (Our Emerald bay folks DO know how to party.) It usually begins before the Laguna Beach show, so make sure you're in place and looking north well in advance of 9:00 p.m.!

JULY

Laguna Beach Skimboarding Camp by Paulo Prietto

(4 camps offered)
(see full details, *Places Locals Go*)

First weekend of July through end of August

Pageant of the Masters

650 Laguna Canyon Road, Laguna Beach, CA 92651
Begins 8:30 each night, prompt
Wheelchair accessible.
Purchase tickets online: http://www.foapom.com/

Try to get any Laguna Beach resident to explain what the world-famous Laguna Beach Pageant of the Masters is, and you will probably find them fumbling for words. I still remember the first time I asked about it ... I had recently moved to Laguna, and was in a cab on the way to the airport. The cabbie asked me if I had been to the Pageant yet. I told him no, but that I was looking forward to it from what little I'd heard about it. The cabbie was immediately dismayed that I had heard so little about the Pageant, so I asked him to explain. He tried, and was so overwhelmed that he started to cry.

Kid you not. This is a true story.

If you go on the Pageant website – www.foapom.com – their own describe the Pageant as "90 minutes of living pictures, incredible faithful art re-creations of classical and contemporary works with real people posing to look exactly like their counterparts in the original pieces."

Uhmm ... ok. So, I get a general idea of what this means. It's an entirely different meaning, however, when you're ushered into the great, stone amphitheater and the show actually begins.

The first time I saw the Pageant of the Masters, my best friend, Diana, was out visiting from Denver and accompanied me. The curtains parted and the first "art piece" – this magnificent grand master's painting, a larger than life piece, was there on stage. It was an enormous expansion of the original art, of course. We oohed and aahed and thought that was pretty great. The curtains closed and re-opened to a new painting, equally as large and overwhelming in its immense size and fidelity to the original ... and then, all of a sudden ... the people in the painting got up and WALKED out of the painting.

We had NO idea that this is what we would be in store for at the Pageant of the Masters. We turned to each other, mouths hanging open, and "got it" the rest of the show. (Thank God the pageant is kind enough to educate the sitting public early in the game as to how a "painting" or a sculpture" is actually put together with real people.)

This Pageant is the only one of its kind in the world. It is a sizable annual venture of VOLUNTEER people and VOLUNTEER painters, craftsmen and costumers who diligently re-create famous paintings, sculptures and statues, from the famous DaVinci Last Supper to Rome's famed Trevi Fountain (yes, live people are "plastered" from head to foot to resemble the characters in that fountain). It is extraordinary.

Each year, the Pageant's theme changes. You can't even begin to guess what images and artwork these people will pull from each year, so just give it up ... See it in person.

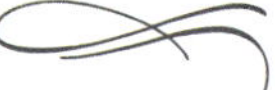

Mid July through end of August

Summer Concert Series at Bluebird Park

About 1 mile up from PCH on Bluebird Canyon Drive (on your right)
5 p.m. – 7 p.m.
Free event

Each year, the City of Laguna Beach shares the musical wealth in its parks with a concert series at one of its more south-oriented parks, Bluebird Park.

This is such a lovely park. Unlike the gorgeous ocean setting of the Heisler Park concert series in May, Bluebird Park is more like sitting in a meadow clearing amidst towering trees. It's quite serene and lovely.

Each year on July and August Sunday evenings, Bluebird comes alive with live music that varies from Grateful Dead tribute bands to great rock and roll, Reggae and jazz.

Pack up your chairs and picnic blankets (not before 3:00 p.m. please) and tote in a picnic basket with all your favorites. It's a great friendly crowd of locals and visitors alike, and a perfect way to end a weekend and begin the week ahead.

Life in Laguna Beach

Our new town "greeter" stands by the original Laguna Beach Greeter, who's now an enormous statue at the beginning of the H.I.P. District.

photo credit to Mary Hurlbut

AUGUST

Mid August through early October

Adult Beach Volleyball Instruction by Kirk Morgan

(see full details, *Places Locals Go*)

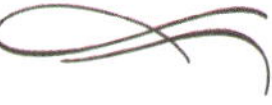

First Saturday of August

Outrigger "Whitey Harrison" Race

The race runs the Laguna Beach coastline

All 32 of the Southern California Outrigger Paddling Clubs begin the most strenuous part of their summer season – the 9-man relay race – in the annual Whitey Harrison Canoe Classic sponsored by the Dana Point Outrigger Club.

This is the ONLY Hawaiian-style outrigger race all year long – on either U.S. seaboard, and possibly the world – that hugs the coastline from beginning to end, making it quite a spectacle for onlookers standing on shore. Normally, this Hawaiian-style outrigger race runs within a quarter mile of the shoreline of Laguna Beach, and it's a show that stops people in their tracks.

The 9-man outrigger relay is one wild race – it's a cacophony of 40-60 outrigger boats racing neck and neck, each with an accompanying motorboat that travels nearby for changes of personnel in and out of the boats. As the outrigger boats race forward, they'll drop paddlers in the water, picking up incoming paddlers on the other side of the boat simultaneously. This is done while the outrigger boat remains at racing speed, which is pretty awesome to watch.

The race begins in Dana Point at Doheny Beach. Women race first, normally turning at Main Beach in Laguna Beach. The men's race starts late morning and normally goes to Seal Rock in Northern Laguna. Get out your binocs for better viewing and pull up a chair at a great location for a rare Saturday morning event.

Best Laguna Beach viewing options for the Outrigger Race:

- The Montage's Cliffside grounds are always open to the public
- The Deck at the Pacific Edge (serving up brunch from 8:00 a.m. to 3:00 p.m.)
- The Hotel Laguna's Ocean View Grill (food starts at 7:30 a.m. but the Grill is open for bar guests just about any time)

SEPTEMBER

Labor Day Pancake Breakfast

Heisler Park, Myrtle Street and Cliff Drive
7:00 a.m. – 10:30 a.m.

At Memorial Day and Labor Day, you can always count on one thing to remain constant: pancake flipping by Laguna's finest. For years now (probably decades), the Laguna Exchange Club teams with Laguna Beach Police and Firefighters to host a $5 flapjack breakfast. Locals line up by the hundreds, and tourists lucky enough to stumble across the event join right in, too.

The Pancake Breakfast is a major fundraiser for the Exchange Club, with all its proceeds donated to child abuse prevention and community your projects.

Girls' Night Out for Boys & Girls Club of Laguna Beach

Event location changes yearly
5:30 p.m. – 10:00 p.m.

The Annual Girls' Night Out draws more than 250 women on a late September Thursday evening. A fashion show combined with a live and silent auction event, Girls' Night was the brainchild of board member Michelle Ray when the Club was struggling to raise funding a few years ago.

The event started with a bang back then, and it's only gotten larger with growing event support along the way. With large-name sponsors, the event location is half the fun. And, silent and live auction items create quite a bit of … havoc … in the bid process. Invariably, some of Laguna's finest restaurants are in place, too, serving up their finest foods and martinis.

Not a bad night to be treated like a queen. The women give back in a big way, though, raising a whopping net in direct support of the Boys & Girls Club after-school programs.

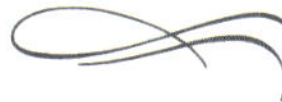

Laguna Dance Festival

Jodie Gates, who founded the Laguna Dance Festival in 2005, is a former principal dancer with the Joffrey Ballet, Frankfurt Ballet, Pennsylvania Ballet and Complexions Contemporary Ballet. Upon her retirement from dancing, Jodie moved to Laguna Beach and immediately noticed that dance was a missing piece in the mosaic of the city's artistic offerings. So, she embarked on creating a dance festival!

Photo credit: Tomasz Rossa

Photo credit: Tomasz Rossa

Since 2005, the Laguna Dance Festival has presented 35 companies, 55 performances, 30 master classes and more than 40 free events. The performers are at the highest levels of dance in the United States, representing American Ballet Theatre, New York City Ballet, Aspen Santa Fe Ballet, the Royal Ballet of Flanders, Oregon Ballet Theatre, BalletX, San Francisco Ballet, Angeles Ballet, ABT II, Hubbard Street 2 and many more.

It's a one-of-a-kind, can't miss weekend on the regional dance calendar.

Annual Marine Mammal Cabaret & Wine Dinner, The Ranch

31106 S. Coast Highway, Laguna Beach, CA 92651
5:30 p.m. – 10:00 p.m.
Purchase tickets online: www.pacificmmc.org/events.html

Photo credit: Wendy Saewert

Given that I have a particular soft spot in my heart for our beloved marine mammals, this is a fundraising event that deserves some serious press. Done in the name of the Laguna Beach Pacific Marine Mammal Center, which takes in sick and injured marine mammals by the hundreds every month (see details, *Places*), this annual event takes place outside, under the stars, at our own tucked away golf course.

The annual PMMC Cabaret & Wine Dinner proffers an elegant plated dinner, rare wine pours, high-end live and silent auctions, grand prize raffles, and internationally acclaimed piano players and singers. It's one great way to enjoy a balmy Laguna Beach night while helping our rescue and relief efforts for seals, sea lions and other lovely mammals of the sea.

OCTOBER

Classic Car Show Sunday, Festival Grounds

650 Laguna Canyon Road, Laguna Beach, CA 92651
9:30 a.m. – 3:00 p.m.

A perennial favorite, the Laguna Beach Annual Classic Car Show takes place at our Festival of Arts grounds (where the Pageant of the Masters plays each summer), with 250-300 cars participating. The event runs 9:30 a.m., to 3:30 p.m., and the cover charge is nominal.

Sponsored by the Rotary Club of Laguna Beach, cars compete for every imaginable class, including fabulous antiques pre-1931; American classics through the '40s, '50s and '60s; foreign classic sports cars; and classic Ferraris, Jaguars, Porsches, Woodies, and more, more, more. For those of you looking to buy a classic car of your own, there's no better place and time as Laguna Beach pulls in some of the rarest finds around.

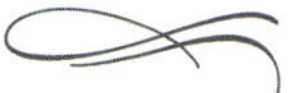

The Buddhist Monks Return: Sand Mandala

Neighborhood Congregational Church (non-denominational)
340 St. Anns Drive, Laguna Beach, CA 92651
Daily

In 2010, Laguna Beach first welcomed a group of five Buddhist monks to create a sand mandala at the Neighborhood Congregational

Church. Little did we know that they would subtly shift each and every one of our lives in the process. Since 2011, the monks have been returning on an annual basis.

This is an event I would encourage you to drive or fly many miles to see. The next two pieces are my original pieces from 2010 to give you an idea of what happens during this extraordinary week:

The Introduction

This has to be one of the greatest events we've yet had come to Laguna Beach (and that's saying a lot) ...

In October, Tibetan Monks will be gathering at the Neighborhood Congregational Church (on St. Anne's and Glenneyre) in Laguna Beach for five full days to create a Sand Mandala in the church's sanctuary.

The Monks will be working on this sand painting each day, from 10 a.m. to 3 p.m. While doors are open to everyone, please note that this is a sacred event, symbolizing their message of world peace and a call to compassion between people of all races and origin.

For hundreds of years, the Tibetan Monks have been creating these Sand Mandalas – what they call "a blueprint for world peace." The Monks will

begin the ceremony with chants, music and blessings of the site to make it conducive to creating the mandala. Then, they begin drawing the line design for the mandala, a very exact and precise work based on ancient scriptures.

From there, they work meticulously for the next several days, pouring millions of colored grains of sand – 14 colors, to be exact – through metal funnels (chakpurs) that vary in size, allowing the sand to flow at different rates. The finished work is approximately 5 feet by 5 feet … and then they destroy it!

That's right – once the work is complete, the Monks do a consecration ceremony to request the continuous blessing of the invoked deities of the mandala. Then, they sweep up the colored sand, symbolizing the impermanence of all that exists … all that exists, that is, except what truly matters - peace in the world, and compassion for one another. About half of the mixed sand is distributed to the audience as blessings for personal health and healing, and the remainder is wrapped in silk and transported to moving water, where it is released back to nature.

A Sunset Excursion with the Monks

As an interesting aside, I was asked to photograph the monks Friday afternoon on a fun Laguna Beach excursion. Their hosts are trying to give them a fair "taste" of Laguna and, with Billy Fried's help from La Vida Laguna, the monks learned how to ocean kayak for the first time yesterday!

National Plein Air Competition

One of the coolest events in all of Laguna Beach takes place every October – the annual Plein Air Painting Invitational (meaning "open air painting," or painting outside). This is a seriously active eight-day festival consisting of 14 separate painting contests, demonstrations and talks.

The artists come from all parts of North America to participate, and they offer friendly, educational tips if you just ask. The event normally starts with all of the artists gathered at the Montage Resort grounds (Treasure Island Park) for a 2-hour competition. They're fanned from stem to stern on winding sidewalks and down various beach steps – it really is a treat to watch them work.

During the week that ensues, I love to see the artists setting up shop in favorite corners, beaches and downtown bustle to paint additional masterpieces. Events include painting days for selected children, high school and college plein air artists. At the end of the week, they do one last mass gathering at Heisler Park to complete the last of a series of paintings. The entire event concludes with a fantastic gala and auction at The Ranch of the very masterpieces painted during the week in Laguna Beach.

This is really a can't miss event!

THE Halloween Party, Halloween Night

Annual Dead Man's Party

The White House Restaurant

340 S. Coast Highway, Laguna Beach, CA 92651

Until two years ago, there have been two INFAMOUS and highly revered PRIVATE Halloween Parties in Laguna Beach. A couple years ago, though, one of them went public, moving from a private residence to the White House Restaurant on Pacific Coast Highway just a block south of Forest. Why the commercial entity? Because it had simply gotten too large.

The Dead Man's Party – the North Laguna Beach Halloween phenom (aka, Shark Bite Lounge) – was created by Bruce White 3 decades ago. This is an insane party, complete with renowned tunnel entrance that tends to intimidate claimed heartier souls.

This fantastic party won't allow you in the regular PCH entrance, but through said famous tunnel from the back alley behind the restaurant. You pay an easy cover charge. Live bands. Special drink concoctions every hour. Halloween costume contests. And the party rocks till whatever hour.

Need a Costume?

Romantic Boutique is your go-to unique solution. See LagunaBeachbest.com for details.

NOVEMBER

Annual Art & Nature Festival, Laguna Art Museum
307 Cliff Drive, Laguna Beach, CA 92651
Tickets on sale at www.lagunaartmuseum.org

Both a festival and a conference, Laguna Art Museum's Art & Nature's is a compilation of art, scientists, environmentalists, marine biologists and big thinkers in a variety of live events (some of which are really BIG events). It's a several day calendar of live art, panel speakers, workshops, special exhibitions and an almost carnival-like atmosphere for kids' events on Sunday.

The event was dreamed up as a way to invite artists and scientists to the same platform in an ultimate push to develop connections between art and science and increase awareness of environmental issues and solutions. As prosaic as that might sound, it's quite an engaging, inventive and fun event, and a jewel in the crown of the Laguna Art Museum.

photo credit: Laguna Art Museum

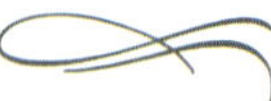

Sawdust Winter Fantasy Festival

935 Laguna Canyon Road,
Laguna Beach, CA 92651
10 a.m. – 6 p.m. daily
Wheelchair accessible.
Service animals are only allowed on the grounds.
Avoid long lines, purchase tickets online:
www.sawdustartfestival.org/tickets
All military and family admitted FREE with military ID.
See also the Sawdust Summer Festival, end of June – first weekend of September.

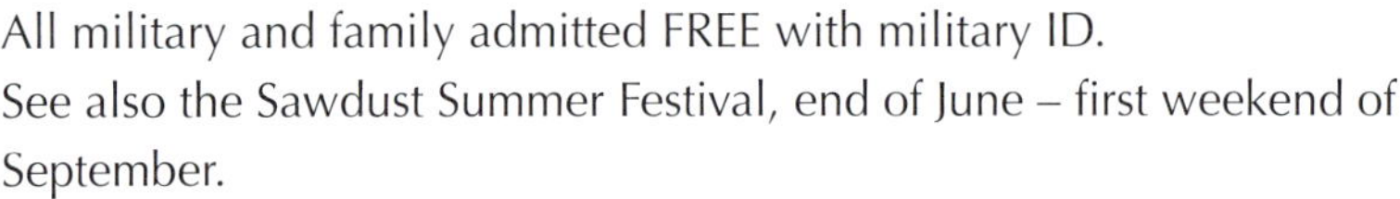

If you're one of those types who buys socks and coffee makers for people at the holidays (yawn), stop reading this right now. You will have absolutely no interest in going to Laguna Beach's annual "Winter Fantasy" because you would find WAY too many amazing, creative and one-of-a-kind gift ideas for the people you love.

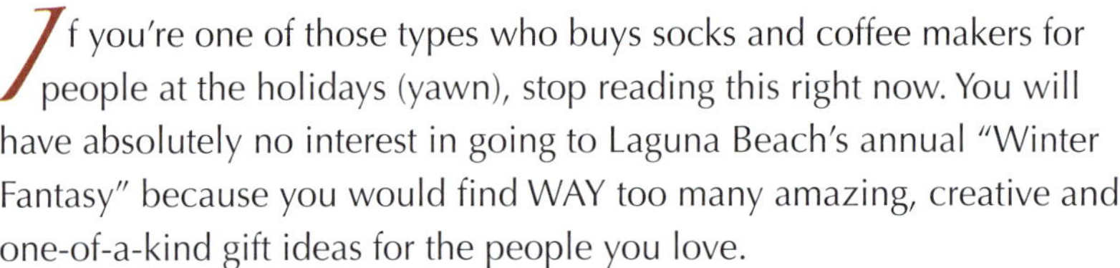

The Laguna Beach Winter Fantasy on the Sawdust Festival grounds opens each year on the Thanksgiving holiday weekend, and remains open through the first week or two of December to gracefully accommodate your very unique and one-of-a-kind gift buying needs.

Honestly, I love the Winter "Sawdust" more than our summer affair, the Sawdust Art Festival (which I happen to like a lot). Now … granted … I'm an admitted Christmas/holiday freak. Throw me under twinkle lights with a hot cup of wassail and there can be no happier human being … but even if you are more Ebenezer Scrooge or Grinch-like in your attitude over the holidays, you're STILL going to find something to enjoy at the Winter Sawdust.

The Winter Sawdust invites its summer artists back, and it adds 30-40 new artists to the festival as well. The great thing, though, is that most of the artists focus on gift-giving items this time around.

You will still have gargantuan paintings and sculptures here and there, but you'll see a greater supply of handmade jewelry, scarves, reasonably priced framed photos and paintings, pottery and Raku, windmills, garden accessories and just about everything else creative under the sun. (I, for one, go to the Winter Sawdust to purchase beautiful hand-blown Christmas ornaments for my clients and friends – they make great hostess gifts, too.)

Aside from 170 different artists' booths in this great outdoor setting, you have a petting zoo, a holiday playhouse (sorry grownups, this is kid-size only), jiving live bands and chorales, wandering carolers, plenty of hot, steamy drinks (along with quality beer and wine), food everywhere and, of course, Santa front and center for all those last-minute, urgent requests.

There's more ... many workshops and classes that teach you how to make cool stuff as gifts, too. Even if you don't possess an artist's classic touch, you and your kids or grandkids can at least learn how to make beautiful beaded wire ornaments (MUCH classier than Shrinky Dinks). Check out the LagunaBeachBest.com/Calendar for updates on seasonal classes.

DECEMBER

Holiday Palettes

During the holiday season in Laguna Beach, be sure to look up to connect with the very roots of our city – nearly 400 hand-painted Holiday Palettes!

Originally begun in 1966 with 104 palettes, these weren't initially painted by our Laguna Beach artists. In 1982, hundreds of resident artists got personally involved, submitting custom palettes with their own holiday artistic creations. Now, it's a contest every year to submit a design in hopes of painting one of the very few new palettes each year. See the full story and details by searching "holiday palettes" at www.LagunaBeachBest.com

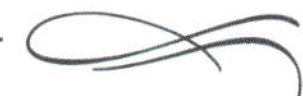

3 BEST SHOPS FOR HOLIDAY DÉCOR

I'm an admitted Christmas holiday freak. Apparently, though, I'm not the only one who thinks it can't come soon enough. These are the three shops I recommend for the most creative and ingenuous holiday décor. For complete details and more photos, go to www.LagunaBeachBest.com and search the names of each of these stores.

Black Iris, South Laguna Beach

Known for their spectacular floral arrangements year-round, the Black Iris'

elves get busy in early October to transform the sop into a Christmas tree wonderland. Shop thousands of ornaments and scads of ribbon from a number of glorious trees.

Laguna Colony, Downtown Laguna Beach

Owner Paul Mosley doesn't buy vast quantities of any item of holiday décor, so people who know Paul's décor don't screw around – they beeline it for The Colony and make quick work of it!

Laguna Nursery, H.I.P. District

Aside from a fantastic array of gorgeous poinsettias at Laguna Nursery, you will find clearly unique holiday décor, tree ornaments and bells and baubles artfully tucked into corners, strewn in table displays and hanging from the rafters.

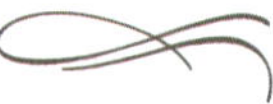

First Monday, after Thanksgiving

The Montage Tree Lighting Event

30801 S. Coast Highway, Laguna Beach, CA 92651

If you've never been to the Montage Resort, this holiday tree-lighting event for young and old is a perfect introduction. Always set for the first Monday after Thanksgiving, the Montage in Laguna Beach does it up once again for residents and visitors alike. This is an event for the record books each and every year in Laguna Beach.

Each year, and days in advance, the Resort selects and trucks in a ginormous White Fir tree for the occasion. One of my dearest friends, Chris Karl, and his team from Ambius haul in the enormous tree, dig the enormous hole (that's Chris testing its depth), right the tree and then begin stringing its thousands of lights. At the same time, the team attends to many palms and décor items inside and on the Resort property for the big occasion. It's a massive job, and the team works tirelessly to create an event that equals this fantastic resort's setting. (See Chris' work here: www.ambius.com/designers/chris-karl).

In the end, it's a spectacular evening with strolling carolers, hot chocolate stations, delectable "finger food" stations, and all sorts of children's activities as we all wait in anticipation of the spectacular moment when all the lights go "ON."

Admission is free, but you can RSVP to the Montage (they'd love to know you're coming) at MLBRSVP@montagehotels.com or call (949) 715-6608 if you plan on attending. The hotel normally offers fantastic room rates for the evening and subsequent weekend as well – just check LagunaBeachBest.com for information as the date draws nigh.

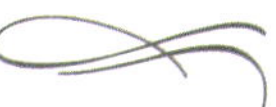

First Friday in December

Hospitality Night (The Santa Claus Parade), Downtown Laguna Beach

Cut from the cloth of an old Andy Griffith show, our Laguna Beach "Hospitality Night" (or "First Night" or "Santa Parade") is about as down home nostalgic as you can get.

On the first Friday of December at about 5:00 p.m., the fire truck sirens start screeching in South Laguna as the trucks make their way through our streets with THE Santa Claus on board (I'm sure it's him.). Meanwhile, the Forest Avenue in front of City Hall and the connected Forest

Photo credit: andrewzelinko@gmail.com

Avenue running straight to the ocean, are both shut down to foot traffic only – and what a lot of foot traffic it is.

From all directions, thousands of people pour into this little section of downtown to see Santa, himself, light the Pepper Tree at City Hall (about 6:00 p.m.). From there, the Santa Parade proceeds as the Jolly Old Elf works his way down Forest Avenue (quite often led by a team of greyhounds) to situate himself in his little Santa cottage. For the remainder of the evening, Santa greets kids and helps them get to the bottom of their holiday wish lists.

Meanwhile, retailers stay open much later, with free drinks and appetizers, and the Laguna Beach restaurants are happily accommodating. Christmas chorales, live Christmas jazz, and popular bands on a makeshift stage get party revelers in the holiday spirit.

Free trolley service always runs along Coast Hwy from 5-9 p.m. (bundle up!). And, yet another holiday tradition is the free screening of "It's A Wonderful Life" at 9:15 p.m. at South Coast Theater. If you're not in the holiday spirit after this event, well ... there's just no saving your soul.

First Saturday in December

Crystal Cove Tree Lighting Event and Holiday Bazaar

8471 N. Coast Highway, Laguna Beach, CA 92651

Historical Crystal Cove is such a beauty with its restored cottages, restaurants and shops. It's even more magical during its holiday tree lighting event right on the beach in front of the Beachcomber Cafe. Sponsored by the Crystal Cove Alliance, the festivities begin at 3:00 p.m., and Santa arrives at about 4:00 p.m. The Crystal Cove tree lighting occurs right around sunset.

The historical Crystal Cove event is the only holiday tree display on the beach of the entire California coast, and what a beauty that tree is. Go to LagunaBeachBest.com for updated parking and Holiday Bazaar details for the weekend in Crystal Cove.

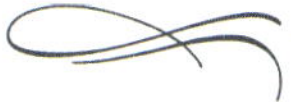

First Weekend in December

Crystal Cove Holiday Bazaar

8471 N. Coast Highway, Laguna Beach, CA 92651

As a kick-off to the holidays, Crystal Cove also hosts an annual holiday bazaar with fine art, holiday gifts, author book signings and craft classes for kids. As "crafts" fairs go, this is a great one as it offers truly sophisticated and unique gift ideas from many of the area's most popular artists. One of its largest fundraisers of the year, proceeds benefit the restoration and education efforts of Crystal Cove State Park & The Historic District. Go to LagunaBeachBest.com for updated parking and Holiday Bazaar details for the weekend in Crystal Cove.

For a complete directory on Christmas Eve Services and New Year's Eve Parties & Dining, go to LagunaBeachBest.com

Places
Locals Go
& What Locals Do
The Ranch at Laguna Beach
31106 S. Coast Highway • Laguna Beach

Many Laguna residents participate in scheduled events (see "Weekly & Monthly Events") but we get involved in a host of other activities, too. As an example … if you love hiking or mountain biking, where would we recommend you go? If you want to enroll yourself or your child in an actual weeklong summer camp, what are the perennial favorites in Laguna Beach? Where would a resident go for Stand Up Paddleboard lessons, a great gym workout, or a badly needed massage?

This section is a beginner's list of hodge-podge activities, interests and favorites places we take ourselves … and our own visiting tourists.

The Ranch at Laguna Beach
31106 S. Coast Highway • Laguna Beach

THE RANCH AT LAGUNA BEACH

31106 S. Coast Highway, Laguna Beach, CA 92651
(949) 499-2271
Hours: 6:00 a.m. - 7:30 p.m.

In 1871, she welcomed the first home in Laguna Beach. Now – 142 years later – she will play host to Laguna's last, great resort.

It's a fitting honor for this hidden gem, who's so reticent of the spotlight that most people drive right past without even looking in The Ranch's direction. Those who have stopped to get to know this sanctuary, though, come away with a memory that lasts a lifetime.

For Mark Christy, it's high time this beauty was introduced to a much larger audience of admirers.

The Ranch at Laguna Beach, in previous lifetimes, has also been known as The Thurston Homestead, Ben Brown's or Aliso Creek Inn.

From the entryway on Coast Highway, you wonder how a hotel and a 9-hole golf course can be tucked back in what seems like such a tiny space. Drive a few hundred yards into the interior, though, and The Ranch at Laguna Beach offers a stunning enclave that meanders beneath towering canyon walls.

"Most people think they've taken a wrong turn when they first turn up our street," says Director of Sales & Marketing Jim Tolbert. "But once they make that final turn and the entire canyon opens up, they're just stunned. The Ranch at Laguna Beach is not what anyone expects."

The Ranch at Laguna Beach is the "yin" to the rest of Laguna Beach's "yang." Not even a quarter mile away, the Pacific pounds its way onto the beaches and rocks, and thousands of visitors create their own riotous color palette of beach blankets and umbrellas. There is a constant thrum of energy and activity in Laguna Beach.

In contrast, The Ranch at Laguna Beach is sublime serenity.

"We have people tell us that as soon as they get beyond the first hole of the golf course, everything changes for them," says General Manager Kurt Bjorkman. "This place just has that kind of way about it."

The name, "The Ranch at Laguna Beach," came just as easily to the new owners. "From Day One, this was "a Ranch," says Bjorkman. "It just had that old-school, relaxed vibe about it."

Indeed, "The Thurston Ranch" was what it was commonly referred to when the Thurston Homestead was established here in 1871. Today, the existing hotel still stands, but Owner Mark Christy is updating the hotel's roofing and siding and modernizing the banquet facilities and kitchen to add renewed sheen and polish to the property.

Nostalgia Draped in Modern-Day Luxury

"If you want to enjoy your honeymoon in seclusion, you can have that," says Christy. "And, if you want your entire wedding party in a series of hotel rooms that converge onto one courtyard, you can have that, too. This is as individualized or as group-oriented an experience as you wish it to be."

The Ranch's original 64-rooms have been reconfigured to 97 hotel units, including 64 large hotel rooms, nine studios, three massive 1-bedroom suites and 20 2-bedroom "cottages" that feature 1,125 square feet in an upstairs/downstairs layout. Lastly, the hexagonal Brown house (now named "The Treehouse") will be included in the mix as a separate, two-story home that overlooks the 87 acres of green expanse.

Even the hotel lobby's location has been changed to create a greater "sense of arrival" for guests.

"I was working at my 13th hotel, and it was a pretty amazing place, but I just knew I had to be here at The Ranch at Laguna Beach," says GM Bjorkman. "For the most part, people in the hospitality industry consign themselves to a rather nomadic lifestyle – movement is normal. But I know my entire career has led to this project. I'm submerged completely, every day; there's just nothing like it."

Adds Tolbert, "Every day I drive up here, I feel folded into the family. There's a sense of commitment here from everyone involved; it's become a real labor of love.

"It's important that we give The Ranch at Laguna Beach a chance to really shine in front of the Laguna Beach community ... and a global community as well. This IS the unique culture of Laguna Beach," says Tolbert.

photo credit: Wendy Saewert

THE BEST, SHORTEST, MOST MEANINGFUL TOUR IN TOWN: THE PACIFIC MARINE MAMMAL CENTER

20612 Laguna Canyon Road, Laguna Beach, CA 92651
(949) 494-3050 (use this to call when you find a sick sea lion or seal, too)

No charge, but donations are very much appreciated.

Tucked away next to our Animal Shelter in Laguna Canyon is our "shelter" for swimmin' creatures – the Pacific Marine Mammal Center (PMMC). It's a very small space that happens to be doing a world of wonderful good for our area's seals and sea lions. It is, in fact, one of the busiest marine mammal hospitals in the state of California, (Given that it was originally started in Founder John Cunningham's bathtub, the PMMC has come a long way!).

When seals and sea lions take a beating out there in the wild, they will beach themselves with hopes that someone will call in the good doctors of the PMMC. In a matter of minutes, the PMMC dispatches its own "critter ambulance" and paramedics to scoop up the sad, disheveled marine mammal and cart it back to the PMMC hospital.

Some marine mammals come in with dehydration issues, while others show up with far worse injury. Whatever the case, the vets and staff at the PMMC begins the rehabilitation process, and a seal or sea lion will spend whatever time it takes at the PMMC to reach full recovery.

As these lovely creatures nurse themselves along and befriend fellow hospital mates, the public is welcome to come to the outside pens and pools for an up-close-and-personal look. This isn't an extensive tour of halls and wings and glassed in treatment centers ... but the walkways that allow full visibility to the seal and sea lion pens and pools is happily entertaining and absorbing. Seals and sea lions are normally frisky, playful creatures, and as soon as they begin feeling better, they're quite the show to watch. The PMMC normally has docents posted outside, too, for anyone's questions.

Organized tours and field trips for a more in-depth look are also available to groups. Just call the center to learn more and schedule your event. And, throughout this book and my blog, you will find more information on fundraising events (see *Events*) and Camp Pinniped, a weeklong summer camp that teaches kids how to care for these creatures of the sea (see this section).

Once the seals and sea lions are rehabilitated completely, they are released back to the ocean. Many Laguna Beach residents are members of the PMMC's Fur Seal Club (See: http://www.pacificmmc.org/membership), which allows us to attend these Release Parties, a series of funny, tear-jerky moments as the caged seals and sea lions get their first real whiff of the ocean.

The PMMC might not be a massive facility, but it has a mighty heart and a bottomless soul. Be sure to stop in, bring a few dollars along for donating, and thank these people for what they do every day for our ocean critters.

BEST TIDE POOL TOURS

Tide pool docents are available on weekends and holidays at:

- Treasure Island Beach below the Montage Resort
- Shaw's Cove in North Laguna Beach at the base of Fairview Street
- Main Beach in central Laguna Beach just north of the Lifeguard Tower

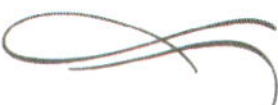

Laguna Beach claims some of the most interesting (and protected) tide pools in Southern California and, with a docent's help, you're in for quite a fun education.

Thanks to our intertidal zones, our tide pools offer homes to a vast number of critters that don't mind you looking at them as long as you don't touch, poke or prod. Because tide pools are fragile ecosystems, no one is legally allowed to remove anything (critters, shells, you name it) without serious fines, but this doesn't mean you can't learn more about this fascinating other world with help from our Laguna docents.

While the docents are certainly hanging out on weekends and holidays to ensure our tide pools remain intact, they're quite warm and friendly to visitors, and offer copious amounts of information on just about any critter you might happen upon.

It's a fun way to spend an hour in the sun, and every visitor or tourist I've taken to the tide pools (kids included) finds it a fascinating journey into the world of our ocean.

CRESCENT BAY PARK

Best Parks

Crescent Bay Drive, North Laguna Beach, CA 92651
(across from the Shell Station)

There are a number of parks in Laguna Beach that are great for people watching (Heisler), sunset views (Alta Laguna/Top of the World) and live music (Bluebird), but the park at Crescent Bay is a quiet beauty you don't want to miss.

Tucked away on a tiny, one-way neighborhood street, if you don't look closely, you'll even miss the directional sign from PCH. The cul-de-sac you'll pull up in is ringed by lovely homes with lovely people inside (ahem) – please mind your manners. Crescent Bay isn't a party park – you'll see that the moment you step foot on its grounds.

The views are spectacular. Your photo opps for the stunning Laguna Beach coastline are even better. The rambling grassy slope is perfect for picnics. And if you wind your way down the walkway, you'll see Seal Rock where – yes – seals normally hang out with their pups on jutting remains from a long-ago volcano.

Insider Tips:
The cove directly below Crescent Bay is renowned as a favorite dive spot in Southern California.

Many locals will grab a burger or – better – a Chicken Teriyaki sandwich at the Husky Boy on PCH, then trot over to Crescent Bay for lunch. Locals will swear that the short walk to Crescent is just the right amount of time you need for the special sauce on that Teriyaki burg to flavor the bun.

Crescent Bay Park

THE MONTAGE RESORT LAGUNA BEACH GROUNDS

30801 S. Coast Highway, Laguna Beach, CA 92651

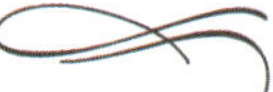

The Montage Resort is our city's highest end resort; it's also ranked as one of the Top 10 resorts in the world. While it definitely caters to international travelers (some stay for 1-3 months at a time), the Montage Resort does a really wonderful job inviting local residents in, and ensuring we all feel welcome.

As you know by now, I'm dyed-in-the-wool and sold-down-the-river on Laguna Beach's beauty. There are few promontories better, though, than the land on which the Montage Laguna Beach was built. This is spectacular beachfront property with multiple beach accesses and rolling, green lawns everywhere. Kudos to the Montage – they've taken a spectacular setting and made it even more spectacular.

Anyone from anywhere is allowed on the Montage Laguna Beach grounds, and residents of Laguna Beach and neighboring guests trot down for picnics, family BBQs, birthday gatherings and more. (It's even dog friendly, inside and out!) Cradled between two beautiful beaches (Treasure Island Beach and Victoria Beach), the Montage also offers easy beach access for its guests and incoming day visitors alike.

I've written a number of related articles about the Montage Resort and its locals-friendly activities at www.LagunaBeachBest.com.

Montage Resort Grounds

ALTA LAGUNA PARK/ TOP OF THE WORLD

505 Forest Ave., Laguna Beach, CA 92651

I just spent another Saturday morning at Laguna Beach's Top of the World (we locals call it T.O.W.) and, frankly, it's an awesome piece of land for activities from sunrise or sunset watching to serious mountain biking, hiking and trail running.

Aptly named, T.O.W. sits at the top of Park Avenue overlooking all of Laguna Beach – get yourself on Park Avenue and simply wind past Laguna Beach high school, continue on Park into the canyon and wind up past the middle school. When you dead-end in that neighborhood, turn left and you'll dead end at Top of the World's launching off point. You can take your favorite pooch on these trails (as opposed to El Moro's strict no pets policy). And, you don't have to pay for parking or possess a state parks pass to park at Top of the World.

... Back to that "launching off point" I mentioned. Aside from spectacular views, you have a wide selection of trails and fire trails to follow on any compass point from T.O.W.'s pinnacle. Experienced hikers and our own Laguna Beach "RADs" mountain bikers will take the more precarious routes on the ocean-facing side, while beginners to advanced hikers, runners and bikers can head out on the inland side. Here, the fire trails are wide and rambling, and primarily lead to the left (cell phone towers destination) or the right (water tower destination). And, there is a vast number of jumping off points from these larger trails.

The fire trails offer a great run out to either destination, even if you choose to stay on top of the hill instead of foraging down any number

Top of the World

of canyons. Just remember – you're at the TOP of the world when you begin ... even the rambling fire trails that seem so easy going down DO follow the laws of nature as well as that chirpy song "what goes up must come... " only this time, you'll be singing the song in reverse. When you turn around to head back to your starting point, you'll find the fire trail significantly steeper than you recalled.

If these 3- or 4-mile loops don't offer enough exercise, you'll find plenty of alternative add-ons that take you down to Laguna Canyon Road (the 133) or, on the opposite side, El Toro Canyon. When you manage to straggle yourself back up to your parking place at T.O.W., you'll find the manicured Alta Laguna Park with picnic tables, a playground for kids, bathrooms and water refill stations. (Alta Laguna also possesses the most beautiful public tennis courts with a view. Try them on a weekday and you'll have your pick of the six courts.)

I'll see you on the trails!

EL MORO & CRYSTAL COVE STATE PARK

8471 N. Coast Hwy, Laguna Beach, CA 92651

There's not only hiking in Laguna Beach, there's SERIOUS hiking in Laguna Beach.

Most folks don't realize that Laguna and Crystal Cove State Park (which includes El Moro) have elevations that rapidly climb from sea level to about 1,000 feet. Granted, you're never going to snowboard here, but you can get a heck of a workout walking, trail running, mountain biking and horseback riding in El Moro Canyon.

El Moro lies just a quarter mile north of the Laguna Beach welcome sign. Our town's only elementary school resides at the base of this monstrous hill and both sit across from the Crystal Cove State Park – a flat, beachy mecca that attracts thousands of tourists year-round.
To the untrained eye, El Moro looks like a friendly set of rolling hills …

and there are many great trails that accommodate beginner hikers and children, to be sure.

But don't let El Moro fool you.

Many of her super-wide "fire trails" accommodate professional football and basketball players in training; cross-country teams; and marathon and triathlon greats. The "park" is a mass of long, steep inclines and rollercoaster hills with names such as "Elevator" (one you definitely want to struggle up instead of down), and "Poles" (a 400-foot vertical hill that some people take to crawling up with absolutely no fear of recrimination).

El Moro also throws down single-track careening challenges to professional BMXers and the internationally known "Radicals" (aka: RADS), a super-competitive mountain bike racing fraternity based in Laguna Beach.

Insider Tips:

- There are no bathroom or drinking water facilities on El Moro once you get past the parking lot and main office facilities. Go prepared.
- Dogs are not allowed on trails. They are allowed on leashes in the campgrounds. Horses are allowed on the trails.
- Campsites are available and can be arranged in advance by calling (949) 494-9143.
- If you park at the PCH side, you're usually charged a daily fee to park UNLESS you arrive before or after the Visitor Center's official hours then it's free! Plan accordingly.

(El Moro) Park Hours:
Mon – Sun 6 a.m. – sunset

How to Find El Moro:
There are many entries to El Moro from the top of Newport Coast Drive by the 73 toll road, from Laguna Canyon (the 133) and from PCH just north of the city limits. The Visitor Welcome Center (with park guides, bathrooms and maps) is on the PCH side, so I'll direct you here first: From the Laguna Beach Welcome sign on the north side of town (as you're exiting Laguna Beach), travel just ¼ mile to the El Moro stoplight. It's a straight shot to the El Moro parking lots from there.

THE ART OF FITNESS GYM & DAY SPA

1080 S. Coast Highway, Laguna Beach, CA 92651
(949) 464-0202

Best All-Around Workout

Thanks to Owner Marian Keegan's perseverance and optimism, this locals' favorite gym and spa is always buzzing with activity no matter what sort of economic year anyone else in town is having. Plus, you have the added benefit of looking across to the ocean when you're huffing away on your treadmill.

The Art of Fitness (or "AOF" as locals refer to it) is a 2-level gym just south of downtown Laguna Beach. Upstairs, a full line-up of yoga, pilates and bodywork classes are offered. (I like yoga with Aviva and just took a body sculpt class with Tracey that whooped me in a good, I-won't-be-able-to-walk-tomorrow kind of way.) On the main level, you have all your treadmills, weight machines, free weights and a spin room. All told, more than 30 weekly classes do their best to appeal to everyone involved in the gym. And, if classes aren't your style, there are a few great personal trainers on hand, too.

Locals and visitors alike are welcome to drop in for day classes, pick up weekly or monthly passes, or purchase a set of classes that never expire (which is darned nice of Marian). The place is super clean and the staff (and even the members) are friendly.

RYPT RIDE (ROWING, RYDING, PILATES, TRAINING)

1833 S. Coast Highway, Laguna Beach, CA 92651
(949) 554-4555

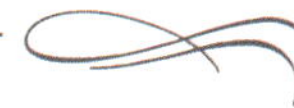

For those of you looking to shake up your fitness regime, I have just the answer for you – Yvonne Kohsel's RyPT Ride Studio.

Saturday morning, I dropped in to my first spin-rowing class combo at the boutique studio, and what a wake-up call it was! Yvonne has amazing spin bikes – Real Ryders – that actually tilt and lean as you pedal. As an 11-year spin enthusiast, and as a 6-year teacher of spin, the Real Ryders were a whole new challenge to the ol' core (exactly where I need to be challenged).

At the start of the class, Yvonne distributed heart monitors to every participant, and helped us dial in age and weight accordingly. While we were able to check our own bike monitors for an update, Yvonne circled regularly, checking up on each of our "heart stats" as we worked our way through a rigorous half hour of spin. Having her there to tell us where our heart rates and percentages should be was an awesome plus – I've been taking spin classes at several gyms and with several teachers and have never had that sort of feedback. It's truly the safest and smartest way to work out, especially for people who are just getting back into a fitness routine.

Just as I was (finally) getting accustomed to the tilt and lean of my bike, we shifted to a half hour of rowing on Yvonne's Indoor Water Rowers. Again, coming from the competitive world of outrigger paddling, this was yet another activity that some of my muscles recognized, but most of 'em were rather stunned to be called into service.

Yvonne also offers Barre classes, TRX suspension and gravity training, and individual training sessions that include reformer and mat Pilates. Additionally, she is just completing her certification in clinical nutrition, and provides fully-ramped nutritional counseling and diet help that combines specifically with your exercise program.

This gal isn't just dabbling in this arena. Yvonne's high-caliber equipment, coupled with her unique programming and 24 years of experience will provide a very effective and safe workout – it's a great way to shake loose your fitness routine boredom.

Life in Laguna Beach

Laguna's Main Beach volleyball courts

Best Massage

LUCY, LAGUNA CANYON SPA

3295 Laguna Canyon Rd., Laguna Beach, CA 92651
(949) 715-0210

The other day, I was out for a quick coffee and ran into a local who had just had a nasty car accident the day prior. I thought, "She needs Lucy," followed by a second thought, "I need Lucy too!"

Lucy Wojskowicz is one fabulous massage therapist and the owner of Laguna Canyon Spa. As something of an athlete all these years, I'm a believer in regular massages and, while I've had some great massage therapists over the years, Lucy tops them all. Obviously, the girl was put on this planet to give massages. She ranks in that rarified world of people who are born concert pianists, Mac computer inventors, Oscar-performing actors and professional wrestlers ... well, maybe not professional wrestlers ... but you get my drift. Lucy has a gift.

I didn't even know Laguna Canyon Spa existed until I received a special offer notification a few months ago. Thinking it was a new place, I thought I'd check it out for my faithful readers. As it turns out, the Laguna Canyon Spa has been tucked in close to the dog park in Laguna Canyon since 2004.

A native of Connecticut, Lucy found her way to San Diego first in 1992, worked her way up to Aliso Viejo, and then jumped on the opportunity to transform the old Laguna Beach Soup Kitchen into a place of her own, a multi-room spa. She initially had plans for just one small section, but kept expanding out and out until her "little remodel project" turned into a rather sizable entity.

Laguna Canyon Spa offers a number of different massages (sports, aromatherapy, Swedish, deep tissue, hot rocks, couples massage (pictured) etc.). After trying massages with a few of her therapists there, I think Lucy has done a great job at "recruiting" the best talent in the industry to this quiet little corner in Laguna Canyon.

In addition to massage therapists, yoga instructors and facialists, the Spa also offers a fantastic pilates room for private and small group sessions.

The Spa also offers workshops and classes in holistic health, nutrition, and conscious living. (These days, we should ALL be crowding into those classes.) And, they carry several lines of facial products and massage oils along with nifty gifts of jewelry, crystals, books, CDs and more.

How to find the Laguna Canyon Spa: When I first tried to find the place, I drove right past it – you've got to look for the moped rental and sales shop right on the corner of Stan Oaks just after the Laguna Canyon Nursery, and turn there (to your right if you're traveling from Laguna Beach in the direction of El Toro and the toll road).

Best Beach Volleyball

BEST BEACH VOLLEYBALL INSTRUCTOR: KIRK MORGAN

Main Beach Volleyball Courts
9:00 a.m. – 10:30 a.m. Beginners – Intermediate (ages 16 and up)
10:30 a.m. – 12:30 p.m. Intermediate – Advanced (ages 16 and up)

Registration includes 8 classes.
Register online www.LagunaBeachCity.net
Contact Kirk: KirkMorgan@cox.net

Given that Laguna Beach offers some of the finest sand courts in the L.A. Basin, it's no surprise that it also offers highly touted beach volleyball instructors for both class settings and private lessons.

For the record, outside of pool volleyball here and there, I thought I had to give up on real volleyball when everyone in my 7th grade class kept growing and I stayed right where I was – munchkin 5′3″. It was a pleasant surprise, then, to come across Laguna Beach's Kirk Morgan, who teaches beginner through advanced beach volleyball classes at Main Beach. Aside from the fact that volleyball folks here in town think Kirk is the Best Class Instructor for Beach Volleyball in Laguna Beach, he teaches lots of SHORT people! Hey, there's hope!

Somehow, Kirk never tires of the "hobby" he's had here at Main Beach on Saturday mornings since 2006. He touts the "volleyball lifestyle" that forges lifelong friendships, and says he prefers teaching Beach Volleyball as it's a lower impact game in the sand for aging bones like, ehrm, his.

The multi-week series of classes with Kirk Morgan is extremely inexpensive and regularly available throughout the year. Check out the Laguna Beach City Guide or contact Kirk at KirkMorgan@cox.net.

LA VIDA LAGUNA

Kayak, SUP & Bike Shop
673 N. Coast Highway, Laguna Beach, CA 92651
Surf & SUP Shop
1257 S. Coast Highway, Laguna Beach, CA 92651
(949) 275-7544

Very few people are able to envision the building of a thriving company around the very passions they love to do daily. Billy Fried isn't one of those people. The Founder of La Vida Laguna, Fried launched La Vida Laguna in 2002 when he decided the corporate world was too drying on his gills.

A devoted water and outdoors guy, Fried turned his love for kayaking, surfing, mountain biking and hiking into corporate adventures and individual lessons. (See, also, Fried's monthly Drum Circle.) Now in two locations in Laguna Beach, La Vida Laguna also began offering Stand Up Paddleboard (S.U.P.) lessons and Yoga sessions on paddleboards, too.

Fried is a fun, outgoing guy who has managed to hire the same personalities to work with him. The La Vida team works happily and easily with corporate teams on games and challenges, as well as with individuals who might suspect they don't have any gills. Lessons out of the beautiful Laguna Beach coves are reasonably priced, and you'll feel a conqueror of all when it's all said and done.

CAMP PINNIPED – THE PACIFIC MARINE MAMMAL CENTER DAY CAMP

Most Unique Summer Camp For Kids

20612 Laguna Canyon Road,
Laguna Beach, CA 92651
End of June thru August (7 weekly camps offered)
Monday – Thursday, 9:00 a.m. – 3:00 p.m.,
Friday Beach Days, 9:00 a.m. – noon

Go online for seasonal pricing, www.pacificmmc.org
Registration: Call 949-494-4050
For 8–12 year olds only

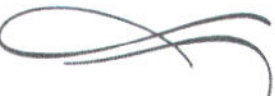

What a great way to witness a marine mammal hospital in action! Each day, a class of 24 excited kids is provided boots and slickers for their experience in California's busiest marine mammal hospital. Friendly staffers and lively veterinarians teach these kids how to rescue and help rehabilitate seals and sea lions so that they can be returned to the ocean happy and healthy.

Each day of the weeklong camp offers up a different theme as children explore marine biology, create ocean arts and crafts, play games and even learn how to make fish smoothies for our hospitalized, dear patients.

LAGUNA BEACH'S (FAMOUS) SURF SCHOOL BY SLI DAWG

Thalia Street Beach
Drop off and pick up: Laguna Surf & Sport, 1088 S. Coast Highway
End of June thru August (10 weekly camps offered)
9:00 a.m. – 2:00 p.m.
Registration includes includes t-shirt, hat, posters, stickers, more.
Registration: www.LagunaBeachCity.net
Students must be able to swim.

Any Laguna Beach surfing parent will tell you – if you want to have your kid learn how to surf, you take him or her to "Professor Sli Dawg's" Surf School, which takes place on the beach and in the waters of Thalia Street Beach.

That's right. Pro surfer Steven Chew and right-hand staffer Nicole Naughton (aka: Nicolian Dynamite) head up an all-star cast of professional surf instructors to teach even the most timid child how to effectively conquer the ol' toes-on-the-nose.

Steven "Sli Dawg" just has a way with kids. He eases kids through the oft-intimidating thought of surfing with fun, progressive wave riding exercises (first on the beach) and helps them get their first start with Softsurfboards for better safety and easy ridability.

Although every child finds a way to master basic and advanced surf skills in just four days, they learn much greater lessons from Professor Sli and friends on safety tips, surfing etiquette, ocean awareness and even their part in ocean preservation and coastal biology with guest teachers from the Surfrider Foundation. The world's top professional skimboarders also drop in to help Sli Dawg's brood with safety tips and beginner lessons on body surfing and skimboarding. And, when Sli's pro surfer buddies show up unannounced for a teaching session, kids are in for a great and memorable show.

On Fridays (the last day of camp), it's a pizza party with surf movies and prizes. Seriously, after years of putting the safest, most fun surf camp together, Sli Dawg deserves a prize of his own.

LAGUNA BEACH SKIMBOARDING CAMP BY PAULO PRIETTO

Best Skimboarding Camp for Kids

Treasure Island Beach (below the Montage)
Drop off and pick up: Public parking
garage adjacent to the Montage off Wesley
July thru Mid-August (7 weekly camps) 9:00 a.m. – noon
Go online for registration fees.
www.LagunaBeachCity.net
All skill levels. Students must be able to swim.

Having followed and photographed the professional skimboarders for many years now, I have to say that the top guys in this sport are incredibly nice guys. Paulo Prietto, though, is in a class all his own. A professional skimboarder, Paulo has not only won three world championships, but he's usually the one winning the "Best Sportsman" awards at all the events, too.

Paulo has been teaching skimboarding to beginners and pros alike for years. He has a number of DVDs and YouTube videos and throughout, he has to be the friendliest, most stoic skimboarding teacher out there. Nothing you do on a skimboard phases Paulo; he is ever encouraging, always upbeat, and terribly careful with his charges.

In his week-long Skimboarding Camps, Paulo teaches ocean surf "physics" and safety tips, and does all sorts of technique teaching on the beach before taking to the waves. He's a hands-on teacher whose greatest concern is that each participant has a great time while advancing his or her skills. Aside from his Solag Skim School staffers, expect to see drop-in surprise visits from the top-ranked skimboarding pros, too.

Life in Laguna Beach

International skim champ Austin Keene recently began offering skimboard and yoga retreats with a group of fellow enthusiasts. See LagunaBeachBest.com for details, search: Austin

photo credit: SusanHeltonRealty.com

Laguna
Beach and Its
Neighborhoods

LAGUNA BEACH & ITS NEIGHBORHOODS

First populated by artists of every ilk, the Laguna Beach community grew up in the 1930s and '40s as an exclusive art colony and retreat for Hollywood celebrities and quiet millionaires. It offers stunning coastline, a mild year-round climate, and plenty to see and do for tourists and residents alike.

Today, Laguna Beach might be more sophisticated with her offering of world-class art galleries, art festivals, museums, world-class dining, expansive beaches and turquoise waters, but her real charm lies in her ability to be both eclectic and eccentric.

There are no "suburbs" in Laguna Beach. No house looks like its neighbor, and, in fact, sleek mansions happily abide next to hobbit-y huts on every street. There are no Big Box stores, and no franchises or chains, save for a handful of small entities and hotel chains that settled in the Laguna Beach community many decades ago and remain grandfathered in.

Thanks to decisive action in the "development years" of the 1980s and 1990s, the Laguna Beach community remains relatively isolated from urban encroachment by its surrounding hills, limited highway access and a dedicated "open space" greenbelt. Nearly six miles of Laguna Beach's coastline is also protected by a State Marine Reserve, and an additional 1.21 miles of Laguna coastline is a State Conservation Area, which disallows fishing and motor boats.

Pacific Coast Highway, running north and south, Highway 133 (Laguna Canyon Road), allowing east/west access, and the South Laguna entry from Crown Valley Parkway allow for the only three primary access points into and out of Laguna Beach. As the Laguna Beach community exists on tourism as its primary industry (more than 6 million people visit annually), expect traffic congestion in the high-season months. Residents who live here, however, find ways around the congestion points, and rarely complain – the majority of them will tell you they live in paradise.

The city has its own award-winning public school district (see LagunaBeachSchools.org) with two elementary schools (El Morro Elementary and Top of the World Elementary), one middle school (Thurston Middle School) and the renowned Laguna Beach High School. Also begun decades ago in a Laguna Beach living room is "Schoolpower," a very successful non-profit education foundation devoted to raising funds and providing grants for more educational programs and top-notch resources for the four schools in Laguna. Laguna Beach caters to several private academies as well.

The Neighborhoods of Laguna Beach

Roughly, Laguna Beach can be divided into 7 neighborhoods or communities. Note, this is a brief overview written from my opinion as a resident. I'm sure Susan Helton (SusanHeltonRealty.com, also in *Recommended Businesses*) will have more concise neighborhood quantifiers, as would several historians in our lovely town.

North Laguna Beach

When you enter Laguna Beach from the north, you're greeted by two exclusive gated communities– Irvine Cove and Emerald Bay. From there, North Laguna continues to extend to Broadway (Main Beach). Locals often refer to North Laguna as "The Tree Streets" as many streets in this quiet section of Laguna are named after trees (Myrtle, Jasmine, Locust, Magnolia, etc.) and boast wide, tree-lined avenues with homes settled back on larger lots.

Home to many of the most beautiful coves and beaches in California, Crescent Bay Point Park, Picnic Beach, Heisler Park and the Laguna Art Museum are all great perches to visit in North Laguna Beach.

Laguna Canyon

From Main Beach, Laguna Canyon offers many of the festival grounds that are so world renowned, i.e., Pageant of the Masters, Sawdust Festival, Art-A-Fair as well as numerous artists' studios and galleries. Tucked here and there, and in larger neighborhoods as you proceed

down the Canyon, are single-family homes, often considered "retro" or "throwback" as they beautifully reflect the original relaxed artisan namesake and feel of Laguna Beach.

Downtown & Mystic Hills

While many residents live above the bustle of retail and restaurants in the downtown quadrant, you'll find many more residents on the gentle hills behind and next to downtown. Mystic Hill boasts the Laguna Beach High School grounds as well as large, rambling homes (most rebuilt after the devastating fire of 1993) with enviable ocean views.

Top of the World

When you continue on Park Avenue past the high school and into the large canyon behind downtown Laguna Beach, you'll find yourself on a steep, winding ascent to Top of the World. (Once you arrive, you'll understand why its moniker.) The only "development" in Laguna Beach where houses might look similar to each other in architectural style (there are still many custom homes here), these houses perch above Laguna Beach with magnificent views of ocean, canyon and inland cities beyond Laguna.

The Village

Roughly covering the inland terrain just past downtown and moving south through Laguna Beach, "The Village" of Laguna is where settlers first settled, eventually building cottages and small vacation getaways in the '30s and '40s. These are rambling, comfortable streets where families (dogs, kids and more dogs) live in cottages with picket fences that seem to want to emulate suburbia but are still too relaxed and beachy to truly follow that more rigorous pattern. As you move south through The Village, you will find larger homes, most of which still harken back to 1970s and '80s style.

South Central

From about Bluebird Canyon, I refer to this section of Laguna as "South Central." Still part of the buzz of Laguna Beach, there's still something of a dividing line here that introduces larger homes on quieter residential streets inland. The streets of Bluebird, Diamond and Nyes Place act as primary conduits to winding, steep uphill drives to larger homes that choose seclusion or all-out glory in tree-shrouded streets or on gorgeous ridges that boast 300-degree views.

On the ocean side of Pacific Coast Highway, "South Central" offers gorgeous homes (shoulder to shoulder) in beautiful Victoria Beach with a ramble farther south to the decadent Montage Resort and Treasure Island grounds.

South Laguna

The community of South Laguna Beach begins just four miles south of downtown Laguna Beach, and is known for being the more "relaxed" side of Laguna. It was annexed to the city of Laguna Beach in 1987 only after many discussions and agreements on keeping the existing community "feel" in place.

South Laguna Beach (SoLag) enjoys gorgeous, wide-open beaches, a beautiful rugged coastline and a quieter hub of retail and restaurants.

Pacific Coast Highway separates SoLag with larger homes terraced for significant ocean views. Inland across PCH, the "original" South Laguna Beach totes large homes as well, but also enjoys a village feel of smaller, cottage homes. More natives of Laguna Beach live in South Laguna, likely because it remains a bit of a throwback to mellower times in Laguna Beach.

photo credit: Mike Altishin, PhotoSteward.com

Recommended
Businesses
LAGUNA
BEACH
LIFEGUARD
DEPT.
EST. 1929
S. Coast

photo credit:
Mike Altishin, PhotoSteward.com

STUNEWSLAGUNA.COM

The online publication began in 2009 with two immediate goals: to provide the community with a paperless source for news and events and a forum to help make Laguna Beach a closer community. *SNL* is nationally categorized as one of some 2500 hyper-local online newspapers and is recognized nationally as one of the most successful in categories of readership and financial accomplishment.

The publication produces two full and new editions each week that are eagerly read by more people than any of the three print edition newspapers in Laguna Beach actually produce for a print run. *SNL* created a unique "scroll" layout with seven different sections that allows the reader to stay on one page at a time for all stories and gives the reader the option to easily scroll to another story.

In 2011, Shaena Stabler partnered with founder Stu Saffer, who has 20 years experience of covering the news in Laguna Beach. Stabler brought a bright and young marketing concept to *SNL* that has led to significant growth each year. *Stu News* has a vibrant social media following and its Facebook page continually has the latest updates on local events, news and traffic. Additionally, the publication has several very popular regular features including *Laguna Life & People*, a weekly *Dining Section*, *Police Beat*, *Where's Maggi* photo quiz and well-read regular columnists.

Stabler is the publisher and is responsible for marketing, advertising sales and the business management. Saffer is the publication's editor.

SUSAN HELTON REALTY

Susan Helton Realty Berkshire Hathaway
2 Ritz Carlton Dr., Monarch Beach, CA 92629
(949) 606-2330
susanheltonrealty@gmail.com

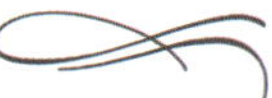

After a successful career in business and finance, Susan Helton's personable fun style led to her natural inclination and interest in architecture, home décor and working with people as a Realtor. Before entering real estate, Susan worked as a CPA and International Tax Specialist, with much of her career with Coopers and Lybrand, one of the Big 4 accounting firms. This gave her the skill set to understand and interpret the financial side of a real estate transaction from a high-level and unique position.

Susan Helton's career change to residential real estate allowed her to combine her creativity and love of meeting people with her experience in finance. Susan provides a professional, strategic financial approach unmatched by her peers, and effortlessly partners that skill with an emphasis on friendly, personal client service that goes well beyond expectations.

Susan Helton is a Luxury Properties leader in the Monarch Beach office of Berkshire Hathaway California Properties, serving her clients in both Monarch and Laguna Beach. Susan's broad architectural and historical knowledge in each location helps home buyers feel immediately acclimated, while home sellers know they've found a true partner who understands the eclectic and unique value of their homes.

VISIONSCAPE

823 Van Dyke Dr., Laguna Beach, CA 92651
www.visionscapeinc.com

After earning several degrees as a landscape designer Ruben Flores still remembers his grandmother's disappointment when, on her deathbed, she scolded him for choosing to be a "gardener" for the rest of his life. Apparently, she wasn't aware of her grandson's lofty aspirations.

Since earning his degrees, California Horticultural Expert Flores has created one of the most innovative, award-compiling landscape design/construction companies in North America. Visionscape, Inc., established here in Southern California in 1988 and based in Laguna Beach since 1998, creates mid-to large-scale solutions that completely transform outdoor environments. From villas in Italy to 4-story brownstones in Manhattan, from Asia to his own Laguna Beach backyard, Ruben

Flores master plans and implements at the "wow" level.

Visionscape, Inc. designs for residential and commercial properties in every possible style – from Buddhist serenity or English floral cottage, to California native xeriscape, and everything in-between.

While the work of Visionscape is year-round, their extensive ability to design to please does double-duty during the holidays, transforming home interiors and exteriors to holiday frenzy, with magnificently decorated trees, and tens of thousands of lights,laughs and smiles. But most appealing is the ability of Ruben Flores, and his Visionscape, Inc. team, to conceive unique concepts and create beautiful realities that invite all to partake in the Vision.

VISIT LAGUNA BEACH

381 Forest Avenue, Laguna Beach, CA 92651
(800) 877-1115
www.visitlagunabeach.com

Given that nearly six million people visit Laguna Beach each year, an Official Visitors Center is not a bad thing to have. Back in 1986, the Laguna Beach Hospitality Association, Inc. (DBA Visit Laguna Beach) was formed as a non-profit 501(c)(6) marketing organization dedicated to promoting and protecting the brand of Laguna Beach for its partners and the community.

Visit Laguna Beach markets the city of Laguna Beach regionally, nationally and globally. You can easily tap into VisitLagunaBeach.com for many of the directories they market around the world, including print and digital versions of the Laguna Beach Visitors Guide, Dining Guide, Maps and more. They are also responsible for the citywide mobile app, too.

Given that the team at Visit Laguna Beach is all about the experience, they offer great concierge-assisted hotel bookings, restaurant reservations and attraction tickets, too. Visit them at the Official Laguna Beach Visitors Center at 381 Forest Avenue, contact them through their website at www.visitlagunabeach.com, or call directly at (800) 877-1115 for recommendations, reservations and assistance in planning your itinerary.

AUTHOR'S NOTE

Created by longtime Laguna Beach resident Deborah Sussex, ***Laguna Skyline*** *is a view you will see more times in a year here than you can believe. For information on this and other originals and giclées from Deborah, go to www.ArtWanted.com/DeborahSussex.*

Thank you for investing your time into learning more about the charmed way of life here in Laguna Beach.

At LagunaBeachBest.com, we're beginning walking tours and concierge consultations for people interested in coming to Laguna Beach. In the months ahead, you will also see an exciting introduction of chef participation and "inspired events" sponsored by LagunaBeachBest.com.

To stay connected with all our events, news, recipes, unpublished shopping specials and more, just sign up at my blog, www.Laguna BeachBest.com, and I promise to never pester or pepper you with junk.

Further, and if you're so inclined, I'd love to have you join our growing community at www. Facebook.com/BestofLagunaBeach.

Thank you, new friend, and I look forward to seeing you one day in Laguna Beach.
Diane Armitage